DEDICATION

To my husband, Steve, my best friend,
Who encourages me daily
And blesses my life.

To our sons, Jared, Nathan, Matthew and Jordan,
Who inspire precious motherhood memories
And continual pride and joy.

To my parents, Wilton and Doris Davis,
Who raised me to know the Lord
And taught me how to live.

Table of Contents

Introduction

The New Testament is filled with timeless instructions that help us discover how best we can serve acceptably before God. Some passages relate especially to men in their roles as husband, father, preacher, elder and deacon. But *What About the Women?* What does the ancient text say to the modern woman about her realms of ministry?

What About the Women? examines New Testament scriptures that specifically concern the Christian woman. It deals with the biblical, love-initialed response from her family, her church and her heavenly Father toward her and her needs. It also deals with her reciprocal response to God and the needs of others in her home, her church, her community and her world. Some questions this book considers include: What seven lessons are older women to teach younger women? What does the woman's veil in first-century Corinth tell us about worship today? How is a woman "saved through childbearing"? Why did the early church care for the older widow indeed but not for those under 60? Must a widow marry "only in the Lord"? How can a wife encourage her husband to be a faithful Christian? Does the Bible authorize deaconesses?

I pray that these lessons will stimulate your thinking about the Christian woman today and show how she can best serve acceptably before God. The ideas considered in *What About the Women?* are part of an on-going study. They are an expression of my best efforts to present biblical truth (John 17:17).

Cynthia Dianne Guy

What About
The Older Women?

Titus 2:3

One morning, as our young son, Matthew, was getting dressed, he discovered that I had put his shirts in his brother's drawer. Puzzled, he asked, "Didn't they teach you better in mommy school?" Mommy school? As a young mother struggling with four children (ages 8, 6, 3 and 6 months), I would have loved such an institution! We were living in California – 3,000 miles from my mother – and I needed more than occasional, long distance advice. If mothering classes were available, patience and homemaking would have topped my list – far ahead of "proper shirt placement."

My feelings of inadequacy were not unique. Many young wives and mothers have felt the need for practical, Bible-based training classes. This is why God wisely provides for such a program in His Word. Titus 2:3-5 outlines a seven-course curriculum for equipping Christian young women to be godly wives and mothers. This passage even specifies the instructors and lists their qualifications. Older women are to teach the younger:

> [T]he older women likewise, that they be reverent in behavior, not slanderers, not given to much wine, teachers of good things – that they admonish the young women to love their husbands, to love their children, to be discreet, chaste,

homemakers, good, obedient to their own husbands, that the word of God may not be blasphemed (NKJV).

Paul wrote to Titus about his difficult work on the island of Crete. The church, lacking spiritual leadership, was infested with false teachers. Christians had no idea how to apply Scripture to their daily lives and were unable to shield themselves from the influence of their slothful culture. In the Easy-To-Read Version, Paul describes the islanders: "Even one of their own prophets (teachers) said, 'Cretan people are always liars. They are evil animals and lazy people who do nothing but eat' " (Titus 1:12 ETR). He commanded Titus to ordain elders (v. 5), stop the mouths of the false teachers (v. 11), and "speak the things which are proper for sound doctrine" (2:1 NKJV). The original word for "sound" means health-promoting. Sound teaching is God's prescription for spiritual disease.

Spiritual disease was rampant, even among the elderly Christians. Paul presented remedies for the aged men first (Titus 2:2), then the older women "likewise" (v. 3). Dewey Fogerson comments on the sins plaguing these older women.

> Even the older women, who might be expected to provide stability and impart the benefit of their experience in life to younger people, were a part of the problem. They had been infected by both the adverse Cretan morality (1:12) and the influence of the "insubordinate men" (1:10) so that they had to be emphatically reminded of how they should behave. Their tongues wagged too much and they were saying terrible things about others. Some of the older women even had alcohol problems.[1]

The charge to the "older" women was to develop spiritually healthy lives themselves so that they would be qualified tó teach the younger.

Wouldn't this first-century admonition be a blessing in our churches today? Young women are turning to radio and television for solutions to life problems but may not rightly divide the biblical answers from worldly ones. Couples are attending marriage and parenting seminars taught by men educated in religious counseling. But even knowledgeable men cannot impact the lives of young women the way older women can – women who have experienced sisterly relationships, childbirth and PMS! Our Father knows best! He planned for older, Christian women to train women in matters unique to women.

OLDER WOMEN: SET AN EXAMPLE!

Who is considered the "older" woman? Paul doesn't specify a particular age. But considering the life skills to be taught, she must have maturity, godly character and experience in marriage and parenting. However, before she can promote healthy conduct in others, she must put into practice herself the attitudes and behaviors urged by Paul. He writes in Titus 2:3: "[T]he older women likewise, that they be

- Reverent in behavior
- Not slanderers
- Not given to much wine
- Teachers of good things" (NKJV).

BE REVERENT IN BEHAVIOR

Paul first calls for holy living. The King James Version reads: "that they be in behavior as becometh holiness" and the New International Version says that they "be reverent in the way they live." The original phrase for "reverent in behavior" is a compound word meaning "to be fit for a sacred place." Her demeanor may be compared to a temple priest, showing a deep respect for God through her actions. First Peter 1:14-16 encourages us: "As obedient children, do not be conformed to the former lusts which were yours in your ignorance, but like the Holy One who called you, be holy yourselves also in all your behavior; because it is written, 'You shall be holy, for I am holy'" (NASB). Galatians 5:24-25 also gives advice on preparing our hearts for holy living: "And those who are Christ's have crucified the flesh with its passions and desires. If we live in the Spirit, let us also walk in the Spirit" (NKJV).

Do you know some older women who fit the profile of reverent in behavior? I asked a group of 25 teenage girls if they knew such women. Six raised their hands. Is it possible that we who are older are hiding our lights under a bushel? Or worse, do our lights not shine at all? So, older women, let your light shine! The younger women need to see it.

NOT SLANDERERS

Second, Paul admonishes the older women to be honest in their speech. The word for "slanderers" (*diabolous*) is translated "devils" in other passages. In Titus 2:3, it describes those who ruin the reputation of others by false accusations. Such lying is characteristic of Satan. Jesus rebuked the Pharisees who were slandering His name in Jerusalem: "You are of your father the devil, and the desires of your father you want to do. He was a murderer from the beginning, and does not stand in the truth, because there is no truth in him. When he speaks a lie, he speaks from his own resources, for he is a liar and the father of it" (John 8:44 NKJV).

Various translations help our understanding. The King James Version renders the phrase "not false accusers" and the New American Standard Bible says "not malicious gossips." While teaching this lesson many years ago, I read the phrase "not malicious gossips" and one lady asserted, "All gossip is malicious!" Spreading rumors is harmful. Someone likened it to opening a feather pillow in the midst of a blustery wind and then trying to gather the feathers back again. The damage cannot be repaired. Before we speak even the truth about others, let us ask ourselves: "Is it true?" "Is it kind?" and "Is it necessary?" Ephesians 4:29 urges us, "Let no evil talk come out of your mouths, but only what is useful for building up, as there is need, so that your words may give grace to those who hear" (NRSV).

We can curb the spread of gossip by not listening to it. When someone begins, "I probably shouldn't be telling you this … ," stop them by answering, "Then please don't. I'd rather not hear it." Many broken hearts, severed relationships and even church splits may be blamed on the loose tongue of gossip. King Solomon describes the talebearer in Proverbs 26:17-22:

> He who passes by and meddles in a quarrel not his own Is like one who takes a dog by the ears. Like a madman who throws firebrands, arrows, and death, Is the man who deceives his neighbor, And says, "I was only joking!" Where there is no wood, the fire goes out; And where there is no talebearer, strife ceases. As charcoal is to burning coals, and wood to fire, So is a contentious man to kindle strife.

The words of a talebearer are like tasty trifles, And they go down into the inmost body (NKJV).

About 30 years had passed since the first Cretans heard the gospel on Pentecost (Acts 2:11) and established the church on their island. Christianity was a still a relatively new religion and unbelievers were judging its effectiveness in the lives of these believers. Did the wagging tongues of these women help or hurt the church's influence? "Death and life are in the power of the tongue" (Proverbs 18:21 NKJV). The older women of Crete were urged to stop spreading spiritual disease and promote spiritual health with their speech. Older women, let your speech be with grace, seasoned with salt.

BE NOT GIVEN TO MUCH WINE

Adam Clarke, in *Commentary on the Holy Bible*, suggests that among the ancient Greeks and Romans, old women were generally said to be fond of much wine.[2] Gordon Fee, a biblical scholar, adds that first-century culture often admired heavy drinkers.[3] We may assume, from Titus 2:3, that some of the older Cretan women were addicted to alcohol. The original word used by Paul (translated "given") is a form of the Greek word for "slave." Other versions state the problem more clearly "nor enslaved to much wine" (NASB) and "not … addicted to much wine" (NIV).

Paul commanded these women to practice restraint in the quantity and strength of their grape juice because they were hurting themselves and their influence. How could they behave as women of God if they were not in control of their speech and actions? Ephesians 5:18 says, "And do not be drunk with wine, in which is dissipation [reckless living]; but be filled with the Spirit" (NKJV). Did you hear that? Christians should be filled with the Holy Spirit, not with fermented spirits. Older women, set a healthy example for the younger, both physically and spiritually.

BE TEACHERS OF GOOD THINGS

Younger women want to know the good things necessary for spiritually healthy personal and family lives. Herein lies a great ministry for older women! Fee suggests that being a teacher of good things here involves "nothing more than informal teaching by word and example, since the content of the instruction in verses 4-5 has to do with being a model, godly wife."[4] Lynn Gannett, in her essay "Older Women/ Younger Women" describes the benefits of such modeling.

> Older women need to be challenged with the old teaching adage, "More is caught than taught." How a mature woman relates to her husband, speaks to her children, creates atmosphere and order in her home, and reacts to the trials of life are all circumstances of life that younger women can observe if given the opportunity. The challenge is for older women to allow younger women close enough to see.[5]

I have fond memories of learning life skills in the kitchen of Mildred Counts (a beloved wife of an elder in our first work in Yucaipa, Calif., during the mid-70s). This fine lady often invited several of us younger women into her home and taught us how to crochet, bake bread and make baby food. During the process, Sister Counts (as we affectionately called her) shared words of wisdom and secrets of life that we were anxious to learn: how to maintain a happy marriage and how to raise faithful Christian children. She blessed us with her workable plan for training the younger, and many of her students now carry that torch.

Formal teaching in the classroom also has benefits. Young women enjoy learning together, sharing problems and hearing answers to others' questions while gaining insights and support from older women. The Highland Park congregation in Muscle Shoals, Ala., has successfully implemented this kind of training program. An annual 13-week quarter is designated for a young women's class on Wednesday nights. Four to six godly mothers and grandmothers are asked to participate as an experienced panel. Students' questions in the first class session are used to create lesson plans for the remaining 12 weeks. Subjects have included making time for husbands, the religiously mixed marriage, spiritual training of children, discipline and combining career with being "busy at home." Each week, the teacher begins with a short Bible lesson on a subject, then allows each panel member to speak. The older women teach good things through Scripture, biblical principles and practical wisdom from experience. The class meets the needs of the younger women and provides a way for the older to obey God's command in Titus 2:4-5. Older women, teach – in a classroom setting, informal discussions in the home, or simply modeling godly attitudes and behavior accompanied by good advice.

TRAIN THE YOUNGER WOMEN

Paul instructs older women first to make the proper changes in their own lives because it is hypocritical to teach what one does not practice. According to Gannett, they must "live lives worthy of imitation." [6] The purpose for Paul's command in Titus 2:4 is translated in a variety of ways: "that they may encourage the young women" (NASB), "[t]hen they can train the younger women" (NIV), and "that they admonish the young women" (NKJV). The original term combines the action of advising (encourage, train) with the kind of advice to be given (sound judgment, wisdom). The KJV expresses both: "That they may teach the young women to be sober [serious-minded, self-controlled]." In classical Greek, this word literally meant "to bring someone to their senses." Fee suggests that in verse 3 "the verb probably means something like 'wise them up' as to their responsibilities as wives." [7] Being a good wife and mother carries moral and spiritual obligations that cannot be fulfilled half-heartedly. What wonderful homes we could have today if young women were taught the seriousness of their commitment to marriage and motherhood!

Considering the prevailing attitude of the young Cretan women, this encouragement to bring their desires under control and to understand the gravity of their roles was badly needed. Fogerson describes the problems seen in the younger women as follows.

> The influence of the Cretan morality upon the younger adults had produced deficiencies, especially in marriage relationships … . Wives were running around on their husbands. They were not being good homemakers. The husbands found that the things usually expected in homes were not there. The women had established reputations which brought disfavor on the church. [8]

Like the Cretans, young women today face challenging circumstances in their personal and family lives. They need guidance from older women who have "been there and done that" and who have learned that the successful way to handle real-life struggles is with godly character and wisdom from above. Older sister, be a mentor for the younger women.

LOOKING AHEAD TO CHAPTER 2

God inspired Paul to name seven attitudes and behaviors young women need. Older women must teach them to (1) love their husbands, (2) love their children, (3) be discreet, (4) be chaste, (5) be home-makers, (6) be good and (7) be obedient to their own husbands. In a culture marked by independence, we may feel it is none of our business how others live. But God commands mature, experienced Christian women to instruct the novices and help them avoid trial-and-error tragedies. In Chapter 2, we will examine the seven attitudes and behaviors in Titus 2:4-5 and discuss their relevance today.

Questions

1. List some spiritual diseases of the older women of Crete. Do we see them today?

2. The original word translated "sound" means _____. Why is God's Word called "sound doctrine"?

3. What does the original word translated "reverent" mean? Discuss some things we can do to let our lights shine in reverent behavior.

4. What is the best way to handle negative information (bad news) about another person?

5. Name some addictions women have today that hinder their Christian influence.

6. In what places, outside of God's Word, are the spiritually sick seeking help?

7. What advantages do women have over men in teaching matters concerning women?

8. Discuss worldly role models influencing our younger women.

9. Discuss godly role models influencing our younger women.

10. How can older women be encouraged to mentor the younger?

What About
The Younger Women?

Titus 2:4-5

On New Year's Eve 1995, our family attended an evening fellowship with the North Davis Church of Christ in Arlington, Texas. My grandmother, Julia Redden, was a part of the senior citizens' ministry hosting the activity. Our sons were reluctant in their participation until someone brought out the dominoes. Then the party began. At the end of the evening our 9-year-old Jordan exclaimed, "Wow! I never knew old people could be so much fun!"

There should be no generation gap in the church. Older Christians have much to offer. Their wisdom and experience are invaluable. In Chapter 1, we discussed Paul's exhortation for older women to become spiritually healthy so they might model godliness and teach the younger women. Seven attitudes and behaviors must be taught: (1) to love their husbands, (2) to love their children, (3) to be discreet, (4) to be chaste, (5) to be homemakers, (6) to be good, and (7) to be obedient to their husbands. Paul had a reason for making these ethical demands – "that the word of God may not be blasphemed" (Titus 2:5 NKJV).

James Burton Coffman wrote, "The world … judges Christianity by the character of the young women produced by the church." [1] How did the young women of the Cretan congregation fare as representatives of Christ? Their conduct reflected a lack of morality and neglect of home and family. They were poor witnesses to the non-Christian world. Therefore, the older women were commanded to bring them to their senses – first, in the area of family relationships.

LOVE THEIR HUSBANDS AND CHILDREN

The attitudes of loving one's husband and children may be discussed together. Older women must teach the younger women (1) to love their husbands and (2) to love their children. Notice the order. Mother and Daddy's affectionate love for each other gives children a sense of security and provides an example for loving their future spouse.

The Greek language has several words for love. You may be familiar with *agape* – the sacrificial kind of love described in 1 Corinthians 13 –"Love is patient and love is kind. Love is not jealous" (v. 4 ETR). *Agape* love is shown when we do what is best for another person whether we feel like it or not. It is the kind of love we are commanded to show our enemies (Matthew 5:44).

But Paul uses a different term for love in Titus 2:4. This is *phileo* love. The word "Philadelphia" (city of brotherly love) comes from the Greek words for love (*phileo*) and brother (*adelphos*). Unlike *agape* love, *phileo* involves a feeling of emotion and affection. T. Pierce Brown contrasts the two terms.

> Agape is not a feeling of emotion or affection. It is a choice of the will by which one deliberately chooses to be willing to sacrifice of what he is and has for the pleasure or good of another. Husbands and wives can be trained to do that too, but this is not what Paul here instructs the older women to do. They are to teach the younger women that they are to, and how they are to show wisely, prudently, and discreetly the proper feeling and concern for their husbands and children. There is no doubt in my mind that there are many women who love (agapao) their children, but need to be trained to … show prudently, discreetly and wisely the proper kind of affection.[2]

Affectionate touch and encouraging words are vital ingredients in a successful marriage. Tender hugs and kisses make a woman feel special. But husbands need affection, too. A man who does not receive *phileo* love from his wife may seek it elsewhere.

The early years of marriage are *phileo* driven. The newlyweds shower each other with affection and undivided attention. But married life brings challenges, and the young wife may soon face feelings of disillusionment. Improperly handled, such feelings can weaken *phileo* love. The experienced older woman must teach her that it can be rekindled.

The story is told about a woman who had lost all affection for her husband. She felt divorce would be too good for him and decided to try an experiment. She said, "I'll be just as good to him as I possibly can for one month. I will not nag or argue. I'll be agreeable, fix his favorite meals, and put love notes in his lunch box. I'll make him feel he's the most important person in the world, and when he's spoiled and dependent on me, I'll leave him." After the experiment, she stated to friends, "I've got the best husband in the world. I wouldn't leave him for anything." After 30 days of *agape* love (treating him right although she didn't feel like it), her husband's behavior changed, and she began to regain *phileo* love (feeling of emotion).

We find similar advice in Revelation 2:4-5 given to the Ephesian Christians who had lost their love for Christ. John writes, "But I have this against you, that you have abandoned the love you had at first. Remember then from what you have fallen; repent, and do the works you did at first" (NRSV). Do the first works! Wives, go back and do the things you used to do when you were dating and first married. Honeymoon actions (cooking his favorite meals, admiring his good qualities, etc.) can rekindle *phileo* love.

One of Highland Park's younger ladies told the class that her husband loved bacon cooked in his beans. She had stopped adding the meat but decided to make the dinner special one night. Her surprised husband whispered to their young son, "This is the way she used to cook them when she loved me." Returning to affectionate actions (adding tenderness, smiles and even bacon) may be difficult for some. We must remember that doing what we should, even when we don't feel like it, is not being hypocritical – it is obeying God. And God blesses obedience.

A revered widow told a recent class of younger women, "Focus on your husband's positives. It's easy to see the negatives. But none of us are perfect. You'll be much happier and enjoy your marriage if you keep your eyes on his good points." Cherish your special moments together: sharing morning coffee, favorite songs, favorite restaurants, etc. Plan to celebrate your 50th wedding anniversary! Older women, teach the younger women to love their husbands!

A child can be fed and clothed *agape* style, but there are tragic consequences when a mother skimps on emotionally sustaining *phileo* love. Dr. Ross Campbell, in his book *How to Really Love Your Child*, details three practical ways to help your child feel loved: physical touch, positive eye contact and focused attention.[3] He discusses a strange phenomenon, called the "failure to thrive syndrome," befalling children who do not receive this kind of love. An example includes children taken from their parents for their protection during World War II Nazi blitzes in London. These children received basic physical care; but because there were few adult caretakers, they were severely deprived of emotional nurturing. Campbell states, "Most of these children were emotionally disturbed and handicapped. It would have been far better to have kept them with their mothers."[4]

Some may ask, "Isn't affection a natural instinct?" Yes, but sinful circumstances, such as neglect and abuse, can destroy emotional responsiveness. When Jeremiah wept over the destruction of Jerusalem, he described the sinfulness of God's people: "Even the jackals present their breasts To nurse their young; But the daughter of my people is cruel, Like ostriches in the wilderness" (Lamentations 4:3 NKJV). The ostrich feels no emotional attachment. An ostrich leaves her little babies. She treats them like they are not hers. Why? The ostrich is foolish (Job 39:16-17). But there is hope.

Albert Barnes suggests that when sin has weakened or destroyed natural affection, Christianity can recover and invigorate all the lost or weakened sensibilities of our nature.[5] Sympathetic older women can help stop cycles of abuse and neglect. Tom Holland writes that parental inhumanity is "a call to godly women to get busy training mothers how to love their children. It is strange that we can spend so much money training people for business and professional careers and give so little attention to the most important career – rearing children."[6] Older women, teach the younger to love their children!

BE DISCREET AND CHASTE

The next two behaviors on Paul's list form another couplet: "discreet" and "chaste" (Titus 2:5 NKJV). These virtues strengthen younger women against indulging in worldly pleasures. "Discreet" is also translated "self-controlled" (NRSV), "sober-minded" (ASV), and "sensible" (RSV; NASB). To be discreet means being reserved in your speech and behavior. Young women must learn to exercise moderation in everyday living. Some need help overcoming extreme patterns in their diet. Others have trouble controlling their spending, especially with credit so readily available. And some have never learned to control the tongue. Filthy language, idle words and unrestrained chatter are not marks of a Christian. Women with careless extravagance and rash behavior are out of place in the congregation of the righteous. Solomon wrote, "As a ring of gold in a swine's snout, So is a lovely woman who lacks discretion" (Proverbs 11:22 NKJV).

The second attribute, being chaste ("pure," NASB; NIV), implies having an innocent mind and undefiled heart toward God. The chaste woman will not pollute her conscience with movies, Internet sites, and reading material that would produce impure thoughts. She heeds Philippians 4:8: "Finally, brethren, whatever things are true, whatever things are noble, whatever things are just, whatever things are pure, whatever things are lovely, whatever things are of good report, if there is any virtue and if there is anything praiseworthy – meditate on these things" (NKJV).

She is true to her husband in heart as well as in action and will not succumb to the temptation to flirt. If she is attracted to another man, she rejects the thought immediately and stays away from him. The old adage applies here, "You may not be able to keep birds from flying around your head, but you can keep them from building a nest in your hair!"

The qualities of self-control and purity are necessary for remaining faithful in marriage, resisting worldly temptations, and developing a spiritually healthy soul. Older women, teach the younger women to be discreet and chaste. You are their role models.

BE HOMEMAKERS

Next, Paul urges that young women learn to be homemakers (from two words meaning "home" and "workers").[7] Two good Bible translations include "busy at home" (NIV) and "workers at home" (ASV). This term is different from the verb in 1 Timothy 5:14 translated "manage the home" (NKJV). Being busy at home requires "hands-on" activity. It takes time and effort to make the home a loving, orderly and comfortable haven for your family.

Many young women today do not feel joy in homemaking. I well remember getting discouraged with the drudgery of laundry, cleaning up spills, laundry, cleaning the bathrooms, laundry, picking up toys, and … did I mention laundry? But a wise older woman reminded me that I was not just doing housework, I was creating an atmosphere in which four young souls could grow into faithful men of God! Attitude is the key. The world tells young women that housework is degrading – that such activities do not make your life meaningful. Ladies, important activities don't make your life meaningful, a meaningful life makes your activities important![8]

Older women may offer helpful hints for turning housework into homemaking: First, we must realize that almost all occupations have boring, monotonous tasks. Helen B. Andelin, writing in *Fascinating Womanhood*, says we must face them for what they are – necessary responsibilities.[9] Second, we must avoid overcrowding our lives. Too many activities and obligations can put us always in a hurry so that we are rushing to do the bare minimum. Andelin again states:

> Many women fail to find happiness in homemaking because they go only the first mile. They give only the bare stint of requirement – just enough to get by. They feed and clothe the family and keep the house reasonably clean, but not an ounce more. Their meals are all "quick and easy," and then they are off to some outside diversion to try to find their satisfaction from life. No woman who ever gave just enough to get by ever enjoyed homemaking. There is no joy in the first mile. You have to give more than is required to enjoy any responsibility.[10]

We must ask ourselves, "If home is where the heart is, does my home reflect it?"

One question often asked by young women concerns balancing an outside career with being "busy at home." Although Scripture does not prohibit working away from home, it does emphasize commitment to family as first priority. An older woman might begin teaching Proverbs 31 where we find a study of the energetic, virtuous woman working far into the night. She may recommend some wonderful books such as Emilie Barnes' *More Hours in My Day* and Sybil Stanton's *The 25-Hour Woman*, which offer great tips on wisely using our time. I find great satisfaction and efficiency in making a daily "to do" list, prioritizing each item, and marking them off as completed. Being "busy at home" without a feeling of accomplishment makes the stressed-out young woman a prime target for depression.

What about the young woman whose heart is torn between family and job? When financial practicality demands her best from 9 to 5 and her family gets what is left over, guilt may consume her. The wise older women can help her evaluate her situation. Psychologist Brenda Hunter, in her book *The Power of Mother Love*, urges, "It would be far better for a woman to follow her heart and find creative solutions to make ends meet than to be torn asunder. Usually it's possible to live on less and, if we are Christians, to expect God to provide the rest."[11] Excellent resources include *Home by Choice* by Dr. Hunter, *Professionalizing Motherhood* by Jill Savage, and *Stay-at-Home Handbook* by Cheryl Gochnauer. Older women, please share stories of God's abundant blessings in your life!

Home and family are gifts from God. Older women, teach the younger how to feel joy and passion for making home special and a reflection of love for family. Unbelievers are watching, and orderliness in our home and family declares to the world the blessedness of Christianity!

BE GOOD

Albert Barnes, in his commentary, writes, "To a wife, a mother, a sister, there can be no higher characteristic ascribed, than to say that she is good."[12] The Revised Standard Version uses the word "kind." Some commentators pair "be homemakers" with "be good," suggesting we must have the right attitude toward our family at home. It is tempting to become irritable and demanding with others as we handle the responsibilities of homemaking. Let me suggest taping Proverbs

31:26 over the bathroom mirror to remind us that "the law of kindness" should be in our tongue. If that doesn't work, one can always tape it over the mouth! The term "good" may also imply activities of kindness, such as benevolence and hospitality to outsiders. Both involve using one's home in Christian service.

BE OBEDIENT TO THEIR OWN HUSBANDS

Paul's list for training the younger women ends with be "obedient to their own husbands" (Titus 2:5 NKJV). Other versions read, "submissive to their own husbands" (RSV) and "in subjection to their own husbands" (ASV). The original word here means to "voluntarily submit oneself to a recognized authority." God has appointed the husband to be the leader in the home. "Wives, submit yourselves unto your own husbands, as unto the Lord. For the husband is head of the wife, as also Christ is the head of the church" (Ephesians 5:22-23 KJV). Why did God designate the husband as head? We will discuss this in Chapter 3.

Submission is an attitude/behavior a wife voluntarily accepts; it is not one forced upon her by her husband. It is part of her love for and obedience to the Lord. Those who misunderstand God's plan for the home ridicule submission, wrongly thinking it means inferiority, being a doormat, or enduring abuse. Not so. It simply means acknowledging and accepting that another person (of equal value in God's eyes) holds the leadership role. Warren W. Wiersbe explains the Greek word for submit:

> It literally means "to rank under." Anyone who has served in the armed forces knows that "rank" has to do with order and authority, not with value or ability. A colonel is higher in rank than a private, but that does not necessarily mean that the colonel is a better man than the private. It only means that the colonel has a higher rank and, therefore, more authority.[13]

Can you imagine the private saying to the colonel, "Why should I submit to your authority? I'm just as good as you are!" No, we understand that the private should not feel threatened or compelled to affirm equality as a human being. This ranking of authority and submission simply identifies different roles in the organization. Each works together for the benefit of all.

God knew that families need order, too. In His plan for spiritually healthy homes, He appointed the husband as authority. Older women who have followed God's plan in their marriage understand the wisdom and blessings of submission. They know that the one in authority bears the greater responsibility and deals with the greater pressures (just as the colonel). Being submissive is not the more difficult role. The husband, as authority, will be held accountable to God for his leadership in the home. But he needs encouragement to lead. For those of you whose husbands are not leading the family as God commands, there is help in 1 Peter 3:1-2. We will discuss this scripture in Chapter 10.

The Christian woman who submits to her husband's authority contributes to harmony in her home. She also models respect for authority to her children. Simply look at the families of godly women who follow God's order. Older women, teach the younger that submitting to their husbands as unto the Lord results in spiritually healthy homes!

PAUL'S CONCLUSION

Paul wrote the admonitions in Titus 2:3-5 because the reputation of the gospel was at stake. Christianity was still a relatively new religion on the island of Crete, and non-believers were watching to see its effects in Christian lives. Paul encouraged godly conduct so that "the word of God may not be blasphemed " (NKJV),"so that no one will malign the word of God" (NIV), "that the word of God may not be dishonored" (NASB) or "discredited" (RSV; NRSV). Spiritually healthy homes show others that God's plan really does work!

Christian young women today desire spiritually healthy personal lives and homes. Those of us who are older must be Christian models and teachers. To answer my son's comment about the misplaced shirts (in Chapter 1), Titus 2:3-5 may be the closest thing to a mommy school we have!

Questions

1. List some spiritual diseases of the younger women of Crete. Do we see them today?

2. Discuss the difference between *agape* love and *phileo* love. Give examples of each in how you love your husband and children.

3. Name some courtship and honeymoon behaviors that a woman might practice to revive *phileo* love.

4. What are some worldly hindrances to purity, and how might a woman guard herself?

5. What homemaking duties require extra self-discipline in your life? What helpful hints would you give for completing these responsibilities?

6. How difficult is it for a colonel to lead when privates will not follow? Compare this to the husband whose wife does not acknowledge his authority.

7. What connection do you see between the wife's attitude toward her husband's authority and the attitude of today's children toward authority?

8. Discuss how order (or the lack of it) in our homes presents Christianity to our unbelieving neighbors.

9. Discuss some methods for teaching the younger women in your congregation.

10. How can you encourage older women to participate?

What About
Submission?

Ephesians 5:22-33

On Sept. 19, 1977, my husband and I were blessed with a precious baby boy, our firstborn. I remember that special night and our amazement at the beauty and perfection of this tiny person whom God "knit together" through us. We were overwhelmed with thanksgiving, and from that moment our lives changed forever. Each day brought new and exciting "firsts" – his first smile, first word, first haircut. And we captured as many as possible in pictures. We have three younger sons, but Jared's baby book is the heaviest. There is something special about the firstborn.

God felt that way too.[1] In Exodus 13:2, He said to Moses, "Consecrate to me every firstborn male" (NIV). Deuteronomy 21:17 says, "That son is the first sign of his father's strength. The right of the firstborn belongs to him" (NIV). Throughout the Old Testament, we learn that the firstborn son received a double portion of the father's inheritance. This coveted position held privilege and authority. But these rights came with great responsibility. The firstborn male had an obligation to lead and protect the family.

Many firstborn sons accepted this responsibility with honor. But Scripture presents some who did not take their role seriously. Esau foolishly gave up his birthright for a bowl of lentils, and Reuben was stripped of his right of inheritance for sleeping with his father's concubine. These examples show that the firstborn was not always the smartest or the most spiritual.

But, as LaGard Smith points out:

> [P]ersonal spiritual strength was not the basis of the firstborn's position of headship or of the privileges and authority which accompanied it. The principle of firstborn was more important than any individual. The principle ensured continuity of lineage both physically and materially, and – at least by design – spiritually.[2]

The spiritual responsibilities of the firstborn were especially important. During the time of sacrifices under the Law of Moses, God chose the Levites to carry out the priestly duties "in place of all the firstborn of the Israelites" (Numbers 3:12).

What does the right of the firstborn have to do with us? That concept forms the basis of male spiritual leadership. We can see how by reviewing the story of creation.

> And the Lord God formed man of the dust of the ground, and breathed into his nostrils the breath of life; and man became a living being. The Lord God planted a garden eastward in Eden, and there He put the man whom He had formed. ... Then the Lord God took the man and put him in the garden of Eden to tend and keep it. ... And the Lord God said, "It is not good that man should be alone; I will make him a helper comparable to him." ... And the Lord God caused a deep sleep to fall on Adam, and he slept; and He took one of his ribs, and closed up the flesh in its place. Then the rib which the Lord God had taken from man He made into a woman, and He brought her to the man (Genesis 2:7-8, 15, 18, 21-22 NKJV).

God made Adam first. This is the reason for man's position of headship with its privileges, authority and responsibility.[3] We'll discuss this foundational basis more fully in Chapter 4.

Eve was created as a suitable companion. Adam was given the firstborn right of authority with its ensuing obligations. Scripture calls Eve a helper (a help, KJV) suitable for him (2:18, NIV). Lest any say this term degrades her, read Psalms 46:1; 54:4; and 63:6-8 and see that God is described as our help. Eve was not created to be a slave, an inferior being, or a second-class human but as a perfectly suited helper to complete Adam physically and emotionally. They made a great couple. From a woman's point of view, Eve had it made! She had a beautiful garden home, a sinless husband, instant meals and no laundry! However, God placed one restriction on her and her husband – they could not eat fruit from the tree of the knowledge of good and evil (Genesis 2:17). But Satan wanted to spoil God's perfect creation. He picked an opportune moment, perhaps when Eve was hungry, and he said to her, "Did God really say, 'You must not eat of any tree of the garden'?" (3:1 NIV). Eve knew about God's command, but Satan turned her focus away from her blessings and pointed to the forbidden tree. He led her to believe the restriction was unfair. And Eve believed him.

Genesis 3:6 reveals, "When the woman saw that the fruit of the tree was good for food and pleasing to the eye, and also desirable for gaining wisdom, she took some and ate it. She also gave some to her husband, who was with her, and he ate" (NIV). Notice that Adam "was with her." As a child, I learned that Eve believed Satan's lie, ate the fruit, then, realizing her sinful condition and separation from her husband, went to Adam and persuaded him to join her. This could be the case. Eve would certainly have been more vulnerable without Adam present. But some suggest Adam was "with her" before she ate.[4] This would not change the fact that they both disobeyed God, but if he was with her before she ate, it presents a failure on Adam's part as the spiritual leader. Let us consider this possibility.

We know Adam was not deceived (1 Timothy 2:14). If he was with her before she ate, shouldn't he have tried to dissuade her? Before Eve's creation, God warned him about the fruit. "And the Lord God commanded the man, 'You are free to eat from any tree in the garden; but you must not eat from the tree of the knowledge of good and evil, for when you eat of it you will surely die' " (Genesis 2:16-17 NIV). We are not told that God personally warned Eve. In the Old Testament, from creation until the Law of Moses, God spoke directly to the father (patriarch) of each family. A father (being the firstborn male of his house) had the responsibility of physical and spiritual leadership. Job 1:5 tells us that Job offered sacrifices for his family. If Adam was with Eve and did not try to protect her, he failed in his spiritual leadership. If he was with her and did attempt to stop her from eating the fruit, she obviously rejected his God-ordained leadership. It is difficult to believe Eve rebelled against her husband, but if she really wanted the fruit, she may have succumbed to her lust against his advice and eaten it anyway. Her rejection of Adam's authority would explain God's declaration of the husband's rule over her in Genesis 3:16.

Even if Adam was only with her after she ate, he was wrong to follow her into sin. Perhaps the shame and guilt Eve now knew compelled her to persuade her husband. Perhaps his love for her compelled him to eat. But he knew better. He disobeyed God's command, abdicated his leadership role, and followed his wife. Hear God's reason for Adam's punishment: "Because you listened to your wife and ate from the tree about which I commanded you, 'You must not eat of it' " (Genesis 3:17 NIV). Smith observes: "The point is that Adam had followed Eve in her sin when instead he should have taken the initiative to act as her spiritual protector. At a critical time in the life of his family, Adam was listening rather than speaking the caution he should have given Eve."[5]

In the recorded punishments, we discover three realities of human life that were changed forever in a negative way.[6]

- Man's work was affected. Work that was a reality for man would NOW be more difficult. He would now have to work very hard, the cursed ground would now produce thorns and thistles, and he would now eat his food by the sweat of his brow (Genesis 3:17-18).

- Woman's childbearing was affected. Eve was designed for this wonderful privilege, but it would NOW be more difficult. God told Eve, "I will greatly increase your pains in childbearing; with pain you will give birth to children" (v. 16; 1:28 NIV). Even with modern anesthesia, many of us have experienced this difficult reality.

- The harmonious relationship between husband and wife was affected. God said to Eve. "Your desire will be for your husband, and he will rule over you" (3:16 NIV). Sin ruined their perfect union and replaced it with tension between her desires for him and his leadership.

Woman's submission was not part of Eve's punishment. The roles of authority and submission were established at creation. Adam, as created firstborn, had already been given the responsibility of spiritual leadership. Eve, because of her created purpose, had already been expected to follow him. John Kachelman, in his article, "The Rationale for Women's Subjection," notes that it "began at creation and is a system that God designed to bring order and unity to the human race."[7] Dave Miller, at the 1991 Lubbock Christian College lectureship, concluded, "Eve's sin is not the reason for female subordination, but an example of the consequence of acting out of harmony with the subordination principle."[8] Hereafter in this book, I will refer to that principle as the authority/submission order.[9]

Eve persuaded Adam to yield to her will in disobeying God. As a result, the already established authority/submission reality of the husband and wife relationship would NOW be more difficult. William Hendriksen makes an interesting observation:

> And now that which before was an unmixed blessing – namely, that Eve, by virtue of her creation, constantly followed Adam – is an unmixed blessing no longer; for now she who, by her sinful example, chose to rule him who at that moment was still her sinless husband, must obey the creature of her own designing, namely, her sinful husband. Hence, let none of her daughters follow her in reversing the divinely established order.[10]

There is a divinely established order. Adam, the prototype of male spiritual leadership, held the authority role in his home. Eve switched roles in the transgression, so God formally designated the husband's headship: "[H]e shall rule over you" (Genesis 3:16 NKJV). Smith suggests, "Male spiritual leadership was God's intention from the very beginning. But in the wake of the Fall, God's insistence on male spiritual leadership was reiterated with a renewed emphasis, about which there could be no ambiguity whatsoever."[11]

Ephesians 5:22-23 tells us that the husband still holds the God-ordained spiritual leadership role in the home. "Wives, submit yourselves unto your own husbands, as unto the Lord. For the husband is head of the wife, even as Christ is the head of the church" (KJV). God did not appoint the husband a dictator but commanded him to treat his wife in a loving and sacrificial manner (vv. 25-28). And he is to lead. If he does not lead, his family suffers. If the wife ignores her husband's God-given authority, she also causes calamity in her home – just as Eve did.

Poor Eve. She gave up paradise and a harmonious union with her husband by disobeying God. I wonder – whenever she thought about Eden – was she only filled with regret for believing Satan's lie or was she kicking herself for rejecting Adam's leadership? Satan still tries to deceive. He whispers to women today, "Has God really said, 'Wives, submit yourselves unto your own husbands'?" We answer, "Yes, we enjoy all marital blessings – love, companionship and security; but we have one restriction. We must submit to our own husbands." Satan counters, "But, what about equal rights? Letting him lead implies inferiority and enslavement!" And just like Eve, many are deceived. They reject the husband's leadership. A man cannot lead if his wife will not follow. Therefore, few husbands are leading their families today.

Let's open our eyes. Even the secular world understands authority/submission order. Employees recognize the authority of employers, privates submit to colonels, and teachers answer to the superintendent of schools. When they do not, businesses fail, battles are lost, and schools fall short. In homes where the divinely established authority/submission order is ignored, friction is the norm. The father says one thing, the mother contradicts, and the children are confused. The tragic results are failed marriages and broken homes. There is hope.

Couples can regain the harmonious relationship of Eden. John Piper writes, "The pre-fall picture of God's will for how man and woman should relate seems to be one of loving, joyful complementarity between head and helper."[12] God presents a recipe for harmonious homes in Ephesians 5:22-33. Here, Paul explains the responsibilities of each partner.

THE HUSBAND'S ROLE

Let's begin with the husband. Certain family responsibilities are placed on the man's shoulders. He must provide financially for his household (Genesis 2:15; 1 Timothy 5:8), raise his children in the nurture and admonition of the Lord (Ephesians 6:4), love his wife (5:25) and treat her with understanding (1 Peter 3:7), and serve as leader of the family (Ephesians 5:23). Why is it that some husbands do not fulfill their obligation to lead? Perhaps their fathers did not provide an adequate role model. But it is also possible that their mothers did not follow their divine directive to submit. Again, how can a man lead if his wife will not follow?

God never commanded the husband to force submission upon his wife but to love her with a sacrificial attitude.

> Husbands, love your wives, just as Christ also loved the church and gave Himself for her, that He might sanctify and cleanse her with the washing of water by the word, that He might present her to Himself a glorious church, not having spot or wrinkle or any such thing, but that she should be holy and without blemish. So husbands ought to love their own wives as their own bodies; he who loves his wife loves himself. For no one ever hated his own flesh, but nourishes and cherishes it, just as the Lord does the church. For we are members of His body, of His flesh and of His bones. "For this reason a man shall leave his father and mother and be joined to his wife, and the two shall become one flesh." This is a great mystery, but I speak concerning Christ and the church. Nevertheless let each one of you in particular so love his own wife as himself, and let the wife see that she respects her husband (Ephesians 5:25-33 NKJV).

The church is a body (of believers) having Christ as the head. Christ loved and gave Himself for those under His headship, and they willingly submit to His authority. In the same way, a married couple is a unit of one flesh and, according to God's plan, the husband sacrificially loves his wife, and she willingly submits to him.

Scripture teaches that the husband's role is based on the principle of firstborn male spiritual leadership. But, just as we noted in some Old Testament examples, this doesn't mean that he is smarter or spiritually superior. We all know women who are more intelligent and more spiritual than their husbands. But God commands the men to lead. Why?

Smith suggests that "imposed spiritual leadership has more to do with responsibility than privilege, with requirement of exercise than recognition of ability."[13] Perhaps God knew that if He didn't command men to lead, most would sit back and leave their obligations to the women. And many women would take those responsibilities upon themselves. God's plan of male spiritual leadership is actually liberating for women. It frees us to fulfill the role He has given us.

THE WIFE'S ROLE

In the home, God calls women to manage, to guide (1 Timothy 5:14). Paul uses a compound word meaning "overseer of the home." God placed within woman natural traits that help her perform assigned tasks. He designed her body for bearing and nursing children. If she accepts the role of wife and mother, her priority is to love her husband and children and create a warm and orderly atmosphere for them (Titus 2:4-5; 1 Timothy 5:14). The woman who makes her family feel physically and emotionally cared for is a successful woman, especially in God's eyes.

She may help provide financially for the family. The virtuous woman in Proverbs 31 was very industrious and hard working. But God does not command her to shoulder the heavy burdens of the family leader. Life is very difficult for single mothers because they are forced to deal with physical and emotional pressures God never intended for them to handle. Remember, God placed Adam in the garden to tend and keep it, not Eve. This does not mean she couldn't. God simply did not give her that responsibility. She was created to help. Perhaps she showed Adam how to pick berries without crushing them. However, the first responsibility of a wife and mother is to love her family and manage the home. If we do not, who will?

In Ephesians 5:22-23, Paul focuses on another responsibility for wives – the one God formally declared to Eve – submission. We must submit to our own husbands (Titus 2:5; Colossians 3:18; Ephesians 5:22), as to the Lord. My deference to my husband as head is part of my service to the Lord. We just read how Paul compares marriage to the relationship between Christ and the church. "Therefore, just as the church is subject to Christ, so let the wives be to their own husbands in everything" (Ephesians 5:24 NKJV).

In everything? Does this mean she cannot balance the checkbook or plan the family vacation? It doesn't mean that at all. A man who wants to control everything is not being loving or sacrificial. There are areas in which his wife is more talented or better informed than he. "Submitting one to another" (Ephesians 5:21 NKJV) allows family duties to be handled by the more capable spouse. What about when spouses disagree? The Christian wife recognizes her husband's headship. He must not "lord it over her" in a domineering spirit, but he should bear in mind her God-given woman's intuition. He must let her be what God created her to be – his help. But, when they disagree, she must let him lead by submitting to his authority, "as unto the Lord."

SUBMISSION TO UNGODLY HUSBANDS

Paul's message in Ephesians 5 was written to Christian husbands and wives. It is easier to submit to a husband who is kind and sacrificial. But must one submit to an unbelieving husband? Yes. God established the authority/submission order in marriage long before Christianity came on the scene. First Peter 3:1 says, "[B]e submissive to your own husbands, that even if some do not obey the word, they, without a word, may be won by the conduct of their wives" (NKJV). The Christian woman who fulfills her role can actually convert her husband! We will examine this concept more fully in Chapter 10.

What about submitting when the husband's will goes against God's? A Christian's allegiance to Christ must come first. When the apostles were told to stop preaching Christ, they answered, "We must obey God rather than men!" (Acts 5:29 NIV). This can be done tactfully. Jo Berry, in her book *Beloved Unbeliever*, offers this advice:

> How can an unequally yoked wife do what is expected of her, in a Christian sense, and still not invoke the wrath of her husband when she must, out of necessity, take a firm stand on scriptural issues? The overwhelming counsel of women who have learned from experience is that she should not make a 'religious' issue out of the problem.

> For example, if an unsaved husband wants his wife to do something dishonest, instead of saying such things are against

what the Bible teaches, she should say they are against her moral principles. And it's true, they are.[14]

What about submission to an unloving and demanding husband? Read the story of Abigail, wife of Nabal, in 1 Samuel 25:2-42. Her husband was a harsh and evil man. David camped near Nabal's shepherds while seeking refuge from King Saul. David ordered his men to protect the shepherds, so he felt justified in requesting food from Nabal. When the evil man refused, David was enraged and planned to kill all Nabal's household. Abigail, being a woman of good understanding and spiritually superior to her husband, hurried to do what was right. Instead of complaining and arguing with her drunken husband, she hastily prepared bread, wine, meat, grain and fruit and took them to David. She fell down at his feet and begged, "Please, let not my lord regard this scoundrel Nabal. For as his name is, so is he: Nabal is his name, and folly is with him!" (1 Samuel 24:25 NKJV).

Abigail was a woman of great courage, not a doormat. She would not tolerate the abuse about to befall her family. She did what was right and saved her family, but she remained faithful to her foolish husband. Her priority was obedience to God. Read how he blessed her.

> Then it happened, after about ten days, that the Lord struck Nabal, and he died. So when David heard that Nabal was dead, he said, "Blessed be the Lord, who has pleaded the cause of my reproach from the hand of Nabal, and has kept His servant from evil! For the Lord has returned the wickedness of Nabal on his own head." And David sent and proposed to Abigail, to take her as his wife (1 Samuel 25:38-39 NKJV).

Unless she must leave a dangerous situation, God will help the woman who remains faithful in a difficult marriage. First Corinthians 7:12-16 tells us that the Christian wife "sanctifies" her husband and may even convert him. We all know of men who came to the Lord late in life because of a wife's faithful example. My father is one of them.

RESPECTING THE HUSBAND

Paul ends his discussion with a word to both the husband and wife in Ephesians 5:33. "Nevertheless let each one of you in particular so love his own wife as himself, and let the wife see that she respects her husband" (NKJV). Consider what happened to Michal, another wife of King David, when she showed disrespect.

We read in 2 Samuel 6:20-23 that David returned from the house of Obed-Edom, bringing back the ark of God, and he rejoiced by dancing before the people in a linen garment.

> Then David returned to bless his household. And Michal the daughter of Saul came out to meet David, and said, "How glorious was the king of Israel today, uncovering himself today in the eyes of the maids of his servants, as one of the base fellows shamelessly uncovers himself!" So David said to Michal, "It was before the Lord, who chose me instead of your father and all his house, to appoint me ruler over the people of the Lord, over Israel. Therefore I will play music before the Lord. And I will be even more undignified than this, and will be humble in my own sight. But as for the maidservants of whom you have spoken, by them I will be held in honor." Therefore Michal the daughter of Saul had no children to the day of her death (NKJV).

Michal criticized her husband for his method of praising God. Perhaps he was not blameless. But her words showed a lack of respect. God will not tolerate such disobedience to His commands. Michal was cursed with barrenness. Let us remember her as we read, "[L]et the wife see that she respects her husband" (Ephesians 5:33 NKJV).

SUMMARY

Sadly, many women struggle to carry out family obligations without male leadership. If a husband does not fulfill his responsibilities, his wife must – whether it is working to pay the rent, training the children, or (like Abigail) protecting her family from harm. As she strives to submit herself to her own husband as unto the Lord, God is her help.

God created Adam first and thereby designed a principle of male spiritual leadership. With that privilege comes responsibility. Satan tempts men to relinquish their leadership position. He also tempts women to reject that leadership. He says submission is degrading.

Actually, it is liberating! It puts responsibility where it belongs. The authority/submission order is God's divine plan, and by acknowledging our respective roles, we can enjoy homes that operate smoothly and spiritually healthy families.

Questions

1. Discuss some possible reasons why Satan spoke to Eve instead of Adam.

2. What three realities were affected by the fall?

3. Discuss Hendriksen's observation that "she who chose to rule her sinless husband, must obey the creation of her own doing, her sinful husband."

4. How can a man lead if his family will not follow?

5. Do you see any signs of "doormat" in the virtuous woman of Proverbs 31 or in Abigail?

6. Where do children first learn respect for authority? Why?

7. Name some issues on which a Christian wife might differ with her unbelieving husband. How might she handle these?

8. Was Michal justified in showing disrespect to her husband?

9. Discuss ways Christian wives can encourage each other.

What About
The Veil and "Authority on Her Head"?

1 Corinthians 11:2-10

I grew up on a small farm in Evergreen, N.C., an area steeped in southern culture. We enjoyed a slow-paced, laid-back lifestyle. It was acceptable to walk barefoot to the corner store to get a soft drink and a cinnamon roll after a hard day's work in the fields. Everybody waved and said, "Hey! How y'all doing?" when paths crossed because we all knew each other. And nobody laughed at our accent or tendency to stretch one-syllable words into two. So when I married and moved to California, I was confronted by a gigantic culture shock. I learned bare feet were out, total strangers did not appreciate personal greetings, and opening my mouth provoked the question, "What part of Texas are you from?" I found it safest to obey the old adage, "When in Rome, do as the Romans do."

Throughout history, culture has affected the way people dress, eat, talk and think. Certain clothing, accessories and even language are symbols that identify one's background and beliefs. This chapter explores one such symbol – the veil.

WOMAN'S HEAD COVERING IN THE FIRST CENTURY

In the first century, reputable women in Greco-Roman and Jewish society wore a head covering in public. Some say this veil covered the entire head with only an opening for the eyes. Others say it was simply a hood pulled up from a shawl. But all agree that if a woman appeared in public without her head covered, she committed a blasphemous act. Why? The covered head was a cultural sign of submission.

THE PROBLEM OF THE HEAD COVERING IN CORINTHIAN WORSHIP

The Christian women in Corinth wanted to remove their veils in worship. But why? Part of the reason may be that they lived in a female liberating culture. Corinth was heavily influenced by the feministic pagan cult of Isis, which gave men and women equal power.[1] And, compared to first century Greek and Jewish women, these Roman women enjoyed wealth and social status.[2] When they heard the gospel, they became aware of religious freedom in Christ. Paul had declared, "There is neither Jew nor Greek, there is neither bond nor free, there is neither male nor female; for you are all one in Christ Jesus" (Galatians 3:28 NKJV). But they misinterpreted Paul's message.

By this time, male spiritual leadership had turned into male domination in many cultures. Women were considered inferior and treated like property. William Barclay in *The Letters to the Corinthians*, wrote, "It is the unfortunate truth that in Jewish law a woman was a thing … ; it was unthinkable that women should claim any kind of equality with men."[3] But Jesus sought to elevate women to their proper place of respect and dignity. His revolutionary teachings on the home instructed husbands to love their wives. And in the religious realm, women were offered a new freedom in Christ. The Corinthian Christians believed this freedom meant that role distinctions between men and women were dissolved, and therefore male spiritual leadership was no longer required in worship.[4] Their rejection of the cultural symbol of submission (the veil) reflected a challenge of authority/submission order in worship.

Do we find such a challenge in worship today? Some still misinterpret Galatians 3:28. Paul wrote the Galatian letter, not to discuss Christians' relationships to each other, but their relationship with God. The message in verse 28 was simply that no longer were circumcised, freeborn male Jews the **only** ones able to have a personal relationship with God. In Christianity, everyone, even those who had been restricted

(Gentiles, slaves and women), could become children of God and share equally in the blessings of salvation. Jesus' teachings never implied that Christianity dissolved the principle of male spiritual leadership. The Corinthians needed instruction on this issue, and, in his letter, Paul presents an authoritative answer.

How did he know about this veil problem? He had received a letter from the Corinthians in which they asked several religious questions (1 Corinthians 7:1ff; 16:17). Gordon Fee, in *The First Epistle to the Corinthians*, suggests they had challenged some of his instructions and perhaps questioned the need for the head covering in worship.[5] In short, they desired to throw off their symbol of submission. It is not surprising. They were an immature group, trying to be Christians in a society saturated with selfishness and egotism. Many had real attitude problems, as was evident in the conflicts Paul had heard about (1:11). Some of these included arguments among the members (vv. 10-11), fornication between a brother and his father's wife (5:1), brethren suing brethren (6:1), and disorder in the worship services (chapters 11-14). The book of 1 Corinthians is Paul's letter of response. The first part deals with the problems reported by Chloe's household (chapters 1-6).

Then Paul begins, "Now concerning the things of which you wrote to me" (1 Corinthians 7:1 NKJV). He answers their questions and defends his teachings firmly and authoritatively. In 11:2-14:40, Paul addresses several issues involving their worship.

11:2-16	The problem of removing the veil
11:17-34	Disorderly conduct regarding the Lord's supper
12:1-14:33a	Selfish attitudes about spiritual gifts
14:33b-38	Women speaking in the assembly
14:39-40	Worship done decently and in order

THE SETTING OF THE HEAD COVERING PROBLEM

Confusion exists on whether these women were praying and prophesying in the worship assembly or in some worship gathering outside the assembly? Carroll Osburn, in "1 Corinthians 11:2-16 – Public or Private?" writes, "[W]omen in the Corinthian congregation are praying and prophesying in the assembly in 11:2-16."[6] Others, however, believe they were praying and prophesying outside the assembly, in private gatherings. Roy Deaver writes,

> The Christian woman could not exercise her gifts of prayer
> and prophecy in the regular public worship assembly, for
> such would assume the very authority which she was for-
> bidden to exercise. Therefore, there had to be another kind
> of gathering in which her gifts could be exercised – meet-
> ings with Christian women (and children, perhaps).[7]

Does the text, 1 Corinthians 11:2-10, help determine the setting? No.
Paul is generally explicit when he is talking about the public assembly.
He uses the phrase "when you come together as church" (v. 18 NKJV) in
his discussion of the Lord's Supper problem (vv.17-34). Also, when he
rebuked the Corinthians for problems with the tongue speakers, proph-
esiers and women in 14:28, 34-35, he used the phrases "in church" and
"in the churches." Bauer's *Greek-English Lexicon* says these terms are
used specifically for the worship assembly – "a church meeting," (1 Corinthians 11:18; cf. 14:4f, 19, 28, 34-35, plural v. 34).[8] None of the terms
signifying an assembly appear in the veil discussion (11:2-10).
Therefore, the text does not show that the women were praying and
prophesying in the public assembly.

We do know that Christian women prophesied in the first century. In
Acts 2:17, on the Day of Pentecost, Peter quoted the prophet Joel, "And
it shall come to pass in the last days, says God, That I will pour out of
My Spirit on all flesh; Your sons and your daughters shall prophesy"
(NKJV). Philip's daughters prophesied (Acts 21:9), but we are not told
when and where. All prophesying ceased when the Scriptures were complete (1 Corinthians 13:8-10). Women did prophesy, but not in the public assembly. It was against general church practice.

Paul wrote in this same letter to the Corinthians that it is shameful
for women to speak in church (14:35). Might these women have prophesied outside the assembly in other gatherings? Acts 21:8-12 explains
that people did prophesy in other places. Therefore, as Everett Ferguson
suggests in *Women in the Church*, "There could be public occasions of
prayer and prophecy where women were the spokespersons but not be
the times when 'the whole church comes together' envisioned in 1 Corinthians 14."[9]

The Corinthians were known for their tendency to debate. Fee suggests, "Some women either were actually praying/prophesying (most likely), or were arguing for the right to do so, without the customary 'head covering' or 'hairstyle.' "[10] Perhaps these women had not yet removed their veils. Maybe, as Fee suggests, they were arguing for the right to do so. Perhaps, they were not praying and prophesying in the assembly but were asking for that privilege. If they thought Christianity dissolved the authority/submission order, they would feel justified in removing the veil (the symbol of submission) and accepting spiritual leadership roles in church. We do not know all the details of the Corinthian veil issue. But it is clear from Paul's response that the problem stemmed from their misunderstanding of authority/submission order.

PAUL'S RESPONSE TO THE HEAD COVERING PROBLEM

Paul began his discussion on a positive note. "Now I praise you, brethren, that you remember me in all things, and keep the traditions just as I delivered them to you" (1 Corinthians 11:2 NKJV). The word "traditions" meant oral religious instruction. Paul had taught them God's inspired messages when he was with them. They were apparently trying to keep God's commands.

After his compliment, Paul went immediately to the heart of their problem and reminded them of God's subordination order. "But I want you to know that the head [authority] of every man is Christ, the head [authority] of woman is man, and the head [authority] of Christ is God" (1 Corinthians 11:3 NKJV).

The three relationships discussed by Paul may be illustrated this way:

(1) Christ > man   (2) man > woman   (3) God > Christ

Notice how tactfully he presents these hierarchical structures. First, he reminds the men that they must be in submission to someone – Christ. They could not dispute this. In the third comparison, Paul presents another irrefutable relationship: Christ is equal to God but submitted Himself to the Father (Philippians 2:5-8). Sandwiched between the first and third relationship is the one in dispute: "the head of the woman is the man." None of these three relationships is debatable. Notice, the three in authority do not force submission. The three in submission willingly defer to the recognized authority. And none of those in submission are degraded; instead, each is honored and blessed by God. This headship order – God, Christ, man, woman – is divinely set. Rejecting it invites chaos.

And chaos existed among the Corinthian Christians. Paul covers an array of worship problems in 11:2-14:40. As he answers the veil issue, can't you just see Paul shaking his head in disbelief at the thought of these women worshiping "bareheaded" in public? Christianity was still a relatively new religion and had enough to deal with without violating local customs and offending outsiders. Appearing in public without the veil declared a rejection of submission. Women who went about unveiled advertised themselves as insubordinate harlots or temple prostitutes. Christian women appearing this way would destroy their influence by bringing reproach upon the church. Paul explains:

> Every man praying or prophesying, having his head covered, dishonors his head. But every woman who prays or prophesies with her head uncovered dishonors her head, for that is one and the same as if her head were shaved (1 Corinthians 11:4-5 NKJV).

The original phrase "having his head covered" literally means "having something on one's head (lit. hanging down from the head, as a veil)."[11] In Paul's day, covering the head symbolized subjection to some visible superior.[12] Both men and women who embraced the Roman religion covered their heads as they sacrificed to their man-made gods.[13] But a Christian man did not cover his head when praying or prophesying (worship) because he did not submit himself spiritually to a visible superior. Instead, he worshiped before the invisible God of heaven. His uncovered head gave honor to his authoritative head, Christ. But a covered head dishonored Christ. Some believe it also dishonored man's own (literal) head because it obscured his male distinctiveness.[14] Wearing a symbol of submission would conceal his authoritative position. Male spiritual leadership, which God commands in worship, would be hidden.

In contrast, a woman who did not have "something on or hanging down from her head" when she worshiped, dishonored her authoritative head, man. How? The veil signified her submissive role. By not covering her head, she displayed a rejection of that role. By rejecting her submissive role, she denied man's authority, thus, dishonoring him. In worship, the two roles must be distinguishable. In worship, the authority/submission order must be demonstrated. Paul continues, "For if a woman is not covered, let her also be shorn [have her hair cut]. But if it is shameful for a woman to be shorn or shaved, let her be covered" (1 Corinthians 11:6 NKJV).

In first-century Corinth, it was shameful for a woman to have her head shaved or her hair cut short (cropped). Paul likens the disgrace of a woman with her head uncovered to one having her hair cropped or shaved. He writes, "[I]f it is shameful for a woman to be shorn [hair cut short] or shaved" (and in their culture, it was), then "let her be covered." Let her put on the veil.

Paul proposed that if the Christian woman would embarrass herself by worshiping without the veil, then she might as well cut her hair short and be totally disgraced. Chrysostrom put it this way: "If she flings away the covering provided by Divine ordinance, let her also fling away the covering provided by nature."[15] A Christian woman should not practice something that is considered disgraceful or shameful in her culture. This destroys her influence for the Lord.

In Corinthian culture, a woman's uncovered head not only showed a rejection of authority/submission order, but it blurred the distinction between male and female.[16] Why must this order and distinction be recognized? Because they are based on creation order and purpose. Paul writes, "For a man indeed ought not to cover his head, since he is the image and glory of God; but woman is the glory of man" (1 Corinthians 11:7 NKJV).

Genesis 1:26-27 implies that both men and women are created in the image of God. But in the context of this issue, man expresses the image of God as authority. Bruce Waltke explains in "1 Corinthians 11:2-16: An Interpretation": "In Greek thought an 'image' gives tangible, perceptive expression and substance to that which is invisible."[17] Man has no other living creature over him on the earth. We see the authoritative act of "naming" in Genesis 2:19 and 23 as God names Adam and Adam names the animals and the woman.

Paul explains that man is not only the image of God, but he is the glory of God. *Theological Dictionary of the New Testament* explains that the glory of God is shown when man acknowledges the honor that is due Him, affirming it by his conduct.[18] Man is the glory of God when he accepts and submits to God's authority. How is woman the glory of man? If man is the glory of God by accepting and submitting to His authority, woman is the glory of man by accepting and submitting to his God-given authority.

Paul continues his message by explaining to the Corinthians precisely why man has the authority role in the authority/submission order. He writes, "For man is not from woman, but woman from man. Nor was man created for the woman, but woman for the man" (1 Corinthians 11:8-9 NKJV). Man's authority is based on (1) creation order (man was created first and woman was made from his body), and (2) created purpose (woman was created for man and not the other way around). Wiersbe writes:

> Both man and woman are made in the image of God and for the glory of God; but since the woman was made from the man (Genesis 2:18-25), she is also the 'glory of man.' She glorifies God and brings glory to the man by submitting to God's order and keeping her head covered in public worship. Thus, Paul tied together both local custom and biblical truth, the one pointing to the other.[19]

The roles of authority/submission and the distinction of men/women were established at creation before any cultures developed. Wayne Jackson explains, "Creation foundational truths transcend culture."[20] Therefore, because culture does not affect the authority/submission order, it was still a reality in the liberated society of first-century Corinth. God's rules for worship did not change.

LOOKING AHEAD TO PART 2
(1 Corinthians 11:10-16)

Paul reaffirmed to the Corinthians that Christianity did not dissolve male spiritual leadership. In worship, the women must retain their submissive role. Because his readers had a cultural symbol demonstrating that role, he urged them to retain it. "For this reason the woman ought to have a symbol of authority on her head, because of the angels" (1 Corinthians 11:10 NKJV).

The original language uses the word meaning "ought" (ESV) rather than "it is necessary." The first-century woman in Corinth needed to conform to cultural "oughtness" or "correctness" to show recognition of godly submission and feminine distinctiveness. In Chapter 5, we will examine the meaning of "a symbol of authority" and the strange phrase "because of the angels." We will then analyze the conclusion of Paul's discussion on this subject and consider the relevance of his message today.

Questions

1. What did the head covering symbolize in the first century?

2. Why might the Corinthian women have questioned the necessity of the veil?

3. What was Paul's message in Galatians 3:28?

4. Discuss the possible settings of the veil problem.

5. Does man's submission to Christ and Christ's submission to God degrade them or imply inferiority? What about woman's submission to man?

6. How did a man praying or prophesying (worshiping) with his head covered dishonor his head? How did a woman doing the same with her head uncovered dishonor her head?

7. How is man the image and glory of God? How is woman the glory of man?

8. What is the basis for man's authority?

9. Can you think of any cultural symbols that show submission today?

What About
The Veil and "Because of the Angels"?

1 Corinthians 11:10-16

In Chapter 4, we began a discussion on the woman's head covering in 1 Corinthians 11. It was customary for women in the first century to wear a veil as a sign of submission. Appearing in public without her veil demonstrated a rejection of her submissive role.

We learned that the Christian women in Corinth misunderstood freedom in Christ. Believing that Christianity negated their submissive role in worship, they felt justified in removing its cultural symbol – the veil. Paul authoritatively explained the reality of God's headship order – God, Christ, man, woman – and affirmed the fact that it was established at creation. He told them that a woman worshiping with her head uncovered dishonored her head. In that culture, removing the symbol of submission showed a disregard for man's authority. It denied gender distinction and male spiritual leadership in the assembly.

Some believe Paul's message still applies and that even today a woman must wear something on her head in worship.[1] Many practice it as a matter of conscience but do not bind it upon others. Unlike the culture of Corinth, worshiping without a veil today does not declare insubordination, blur distinction between the sexes, or bring reproach upon the church. Worshiping "bareheaded," in our culture, does not disgrace a woman, nor does it dishonor man. The veil is not a cultural symbol of submission today and, therefore, is not necessary. Does modern man dishonor Christ by worshiping with his head uncovered? It is certainly a deeply rooted tradition in some parts of our country for men to remove their hats during prayer. You will find many removing their hats during the national anthem or Pledge of Allegiance to show respect. If a man keeps his hat on during prayer, do those around him presume him disrespectful? If so, he is culturally pressed to remove his hat. In the same way, culture compelled the Corinthian women to wear a head covering during worship.

Some ask why Paul did not here condemn women praying and prophesying in the worship assembly. First of all, we are not told that these women were in the assembly. Second, we do not know whether they were actually removing their veils or simply arguing for the right to do so. Their desire to "throw off" the veil showed a deeper desire to throw off the limitations of woman's submission. By telling them to retain their veils, Paul was telling them to remain in their role.

For a Corinthian woman, it was shameful to worship with her head uncovered. So, Paul says, if she removes the veil, she might as well cut her hair short and be totally disgraced. "For if a woman is not covered, let her also be shorn [have her hair cut]. But if it is shameful for a woman to be shorn or shaved, let her be covered" (1 Corinthians 11:6 NKJV).

In our culture, it is not shameful for a woman to have short hair. People do not assume she is a harlot or an adulteress, as in Paul's day. However, certain things she might wear do advertise her as such. If such dress raises a red flag on her character, should a Christian woman dress this way? Of course not! She shouldn't want to send the wrong message. That is precisely Paul's point. The Christian women of Corinth were told that they ought to wear the veil to avoid the appearance of insubordination. And we, as Christian women, ought also to consider how we appear. If something is shameful in our culture and would weaken our Christian influence, we ought to avoid it. We must also be careful not to conceal or appear to reject any of God's principles, including our submissive role.

In our culture, wearing a husband's name is a sign that a woman respects his authority. Promising to obey him as part of the marriage ceremony is a public acknowledgement. Why do some reject these cultural symbols? Might it appear as a rejection of the husband's headship? What other cultural symbols do we have that demonstrate God's headship order in the home and in worship?

First Corinthians 11:7-9 teaches that the distinction between man and woman should be apparent in their worship. "For a man indeed ought not to cover his head, since he is the image and glory of God; but woman is the glory of man. For man is not from woman, but woman from man. Nor was man created for the woman, but woman for the man" (NKJV).

First Corinthians 11:8-9 explains the reason for man's authoritative role: (1) creation order and (2) created purpose. LaGard Smith explains:

> Male spiritual leadership is tied to the principle of firstborn, which itself grew out of the 'firstcreated' status of Adam. It is tied with responsibility of spiritual protection for the woman, who was made to be the perfect match for man. Before there was a veil, before there was a worship service, before there was a culture in which customs could be established, man was the designated spiritual head of his wife – both in the marriage relationship and in their relationship to God.[2]

The message is clear. However, God does not force submission. We are free moral agents. We can choose to obey God and receive His blessings, or disobey God and accept the consequences. Verse 10 of 1 Corinthians 11, where we ended Chapter 4, may better explain the latter. "For this reason the woman ought to have a symbol of authority on her head, because of the angels" (NKJV).

W. Gerald Kendrick, in *The Bible Translator*, remarks on the interpretation of this verse. "The meaning of each individual word is clear, yet how to determine what the sentence says as a whole, and to interpret it in its context, is widely regarded as one of the most difficult problems of the New Testament."[3] The original language does not include the words "a symbol of." It simply says she ought to have authority on her head.

AUTHORITY ON HER HEAD

The Greek word translated "authority" in 1 Corinthians 11:10 has been examined in its various senses. It can mean power, liberty or authority.

• *Power.* The KJV reads, "For this cause ought the woman to have power on her head." Some who prefer this meaning quote Sir William Ramsey:

> In Oriental lands the veil is the power and honour and dignity of the woman. With the veil on her head she can go anywhere in security and profound respect. But without the veil the woman is a thing of nought, whom anyone may insult. ... A woman's authority and dignity vanish along with the all-covering veil that she discards.[4]

His interpretation is that this first-century woman ought to keep control (power) over her dignity and respect by wearing the veil. Albert Barnes states:

> Most commentaries agree that it means a veil, though some think ... that it is called power to denote the veil which was worn by married women, which indicated the superiority of the married woman to the maiden. ... There can, perhaps, be no doubt that the word "power" [KJV] has reference to a veil, or to a covering for the head; but why it is called power I confess I do not understand.[5]

• *Liberty.* Fee suggests Paul may have played on the meaning of liberty because the Corinthians boasted about their new liberty in Christ, using the same word (1 Corinthians 6:12). In 8:9, Paul used the word in warning: "[B]eware, lest somehow this liberty of yours become a stumbling block to those who are weak" (NKJV). Fee says that when Paul writes that "the woman ought to have liberty on her head," he is confirming their liberty to wear the veil or not to wear the veil but that "they should exercise that authority in the proper way – by maintaining the custom of being 'covered.' "[6] This would be like Paul having the liberty to eat meat but choosing not to because it would offend some. In other words, the women ought to wear the veil and avoid offending others.

• *Authority.* Many translators render the meaning that she should show authority on her head. But man has authority. Shouldn't she show "submission" on her head? *The Pulpit Commentary* presents a unique sense of the word, "The simplest answer is that just as the word 'kingdom' in Greek may be used for 'a crown', so 'authority' may mean 'a sign of authority' (Revised Version), or 'a covering, in sign that she is under the power of her husband' (Authorized Version, margin)."[7] The NKJV translates the secondary sense, "For this reason the woman ought to have a symbol of authority on her head" (1 Corinthians 11:10). The RSV names that symbol, "That is why a woman ought to have a veil on her head." In other words, she ought to wear the cultural symbol showing she was under the authority of someone.

First Corinthians 11:10 is difficult to interpret precisely. However, Paul's message is clear that the Corinthian Christian women ought to wear the veil in worship. By using the Greek word for "ought " (and not the one for "it is necessary"), Paul appealed to their sense of moral obligation and propriety in their culture. Likewise, women today ought to practice whatever cultural designations they have that show acknowledgement of submission.

BECAUSE OF THE ANGELS

The final phrase in 1 Corinthians 11:10, "because of the angels," is also difficult to interpret precisely. There are three main interpretations.

• *Interpretation No. 1*. Some suggest that this verse cautions women not to offend angels who watch our activities in this world (1 Corinthians 4:9; 6:3; Ephesians 3:10; 1 Timothy 3:16; Hebrews 1:14). Robertson writes, "The meaning is plain. If a woman thinks lightly of shocking men, she must remember that she will also be shocking the angels, who of course are present at public worship."[8] *The Pulpit Commentary* says, "[T]he meaning seems to be ... out of respect and reverence for the holy angels, who are always invisibly present in the Christian assemblies."[9] Barnes adds, "[B]ecause the angels of God are witnesses of your public worship, (Heb.i.14,) and because they know and appreciate the propriety of subordination and order in public assemblies."[10]

• *Interpretation No. 2*. Others believe Paul warns the Corinthian women not to be like the rebellious angels who refused to remain in their submissive role. Jude 6 and 2 Peter 2:4 warn us that these wicked angels have been punished. Coffman writes:

> The simplest explanation (since Paul was speaking of the subordination of woman) is that this is a reminder that the

"angels who kept not their first estate" lost heaven; and it is not far-fetched to draw the analogy that those precious angels called women should not go beyond the limitations imposed upon them by their creation."[11]

• *Interpretation No. 3.* Barclay wrote that Paul meant a "bare-faced" woman might cause angels to lust after her. "It is not certain what this means, but quite probably it goes back to the strange old story in Genesis 6:1 and 2 which tells how the angels fell a prey to the charms of mortal women and so sinned."[12] Robertson states that Paul was not referring to angels because (1) the phrase "the angels" always denotes good angels in the New Testament (1 Corinthians 13:1; Matthew 13:49; 25:31; Luke 16:22; Hebrews 1:4-5) and (2) it is "somewhat childish" to suppose "that a veil hides a human face from angels, or that public worship would be the only occasion when an unveiled woman might lead angels into temptation."[13]

Dan Owen offers insight combining the second and third opinions. Understanding that the Jews of the intertestamental period believed the "sons of God" (Watchers) in Genesis 6 were fallen angels, he suggests Paul is making "a likely reference to the Jewish traditions about the Watchers who lusted after women who 'adorned their heads and faces to deceive the mind,' as described in the Testament of Reuben 5:1ff."[14] Owen continues, "If this is what Paul had in mind, then he (like the Testament of Reuben) takes a lesson from the fall of the angels that applies to the way women dress and act."[15]

Which interpretation is correct? Kenneth T. Wilson gives good advice about the entire discussion, "Because of the controversial and difficult nature of this section, any interpretation must be held with a certain degree of caution."[16]

MUTUAL DEPENDENCE

In case the men should become puffed up about their authoritative role, Paul reminded them that men and women are dependent on each other. "Nevertheless, neither is man independent of woman, nor woman independent of man, in the Lord. For as woman came from man, even so man also comes through woman; but all things are from God" (1 Corinthians 11:11-12 NKJV).

Men who think their role gives them dictatorship and license to abuse are reminded that man needs woman. She deserves to be treated with respect and understanding (Ephesians 5:25-33; 1 Peter 3:7). Yes, the first woman came from a man's body (Adam's), but man's continued existence comes through woman's body (birth). And all things are from God. Neither man nor woman is independent "in the Lord." When a man is obedient to God and treats his wife properly, submission is easier for her. Conversely, history shows that when Christian women obey God, men more readily respect them. Coffman reminds us:

> Wherever Christianity has gone, women have been lifted up. … [T]hrough the centuries, those societies in which women have honored this divine injunction [submission] have invariably elevated women to higher and higher places of honor, respect, and protection. In many cultures where this ethic is dishonored, women have ultimately been reduced to the status of chattels, as they were in the pagan culture of Paul's day. The behavior here enjoined proved to be the way up for womankind; and the opposite of it will doubtless prove to be the way down.[17]

Robertson suggests that "in the Lord" here means "it is only in the Christian sphere that woman's rights are duly respected."[18] There was a time in our country, when we were truly a Christian nation. Men treated women with great respect. A man would give up his seat for her. He chose his words more carefully and stood when she approached. "Ladies first" was the rule. We still find such behavior, especially among Christians. But truthfully, the women's liberation movement has pulled us down from our honored position – in order to make men and women equal. An old commercial declared, "You've come a long way, baby." Yes, but in what direction?

Paul has made his point. Now, he asks, "Judge for yourselves: is it proper for a woman to pray to God with her head unveiled?" (1 Corinthians 11:13 NRSV). He asked them to determine among themselves whether it was appropriate (respectable) for a woman to worship unveiled. Obviously, in their culture, it was not. Usually the Greek word for "pray" stands alone because it is understood to whom we pray. But

Paul added the words "to God." He wanted these women to realize that, in worship, they stand in the presence of the Almighty. And by removing the veil, they declared a rejection of His headship order.

DISTINCTION BETWEEN MALE AND FEMALE

In Corinthian culture, the head covering demonstrated not only a submissive heart but also a distinction between male and female. In the Old Testament, we read that God required the two sexes to be distinguishable. "A woman shall not wear anything that pertains to a man, nor shall a man put on a woman's garment, for all who do so are an abomination to the Lord your God" (Deuteronomy 22:5 NKJV).

In our first ministry (Yucaipa, Calif., 1975-80), a dear older sister believed it was improper for women to wear pants in church. Although many of us did not believe it was wrong, we loved her too much to offend her. So we did not wear pants in the assembly. Today, pants are culturally acceptable, but shouldn't they still reflect the feminine distinction God desires? Is any attire still fundamentally feminine? There was a time when only women wore necklaces, earrings and pink sweaters. At one time, only men wore tailored suits.

Today, it is hard to define "feminine only" and "masculine only" apparel. Is God pleased with a unisex society? Paul's next words may provide insight. "Does not even nature itself teach you that if a man has long hair, it is a dishonor to him? But [in contrast] if a woman has long hair, it is a glory to her; for her hair is given to her for a covering" (1 Corinthians 11:14-15 NKJV).

God created a natural distinction between male and female – hair length. Generally, throughout history, people have recognized long hair for women and shorter hair for men. In Jewish custom, it was only under a special Nazirite vow that a man put not a razor to his head (Numbers 6:5). Absalom, son of David, was known for his long hair. But he was also known for his rebellious attitude. This same rebellious attitude was characteristic of the 1960s when many young men let their hair grow. Yet, the distinction was still apparent. When Sonny Bono wore his hair to the shoulders, Cher wore hers down to her waist. The phrase "long hair" is relative. Wiersbe states:

Nowhere does the Bible tell us how long our hair should be. It simply states that there ought to be a noticeable difference between the length of the men's hair and the women's hair so that there is no confusion of the sexes. ... It is shameful for the man to look like a woman or the woman to look like a man.

The woman's long hair is her glory, and it is given to her "instead of a covering" (literal translation). In other words, if local custom does not dictate a head-covering, her long hair can be that covering."[19]

Paul ended his discussion. However, knowing that the Corinthians liked to debate, he reminded them that removing the head covering was not practiced in other congregations. "But if anyone seems to be contentious, we have no such custom, nor do the churches of God" (1 Corinthians 11:16 NKJV).

Paul told the Corinthian women that they ought to wear the customary veil. It was the cultural expression of authority/submission order and male/female distinction. In our culture, the veil is not a symbol of either. Worshiping without it does not imply that we reject male spiritual leadership. It does not bring reproach upon the church or weaken our witness for Christ. Therefore, women today are not required to wear the veil, a hat or any artificial head covering.

We are required to do what is normal in our culture to show that we acknowledge the authority/submission principle. In the home and in worship, male spiritual leadership should be seen. We have mentioned wearing the husband's name and promising to obey in the wedding ceremony as cultural signs of submission to one's husband. But what about in worship? Rick Simmons suggested, "If a symbol is to be maintained, a suitable alternative to the wearing of head coverings could be the presence of a male leader in the services in which women participate."[20] We will explore this in Chapter 6.

My husband and I spent 16 years in California, so I had plenty of time to adjust to the cultural changes. When we returned to the South in 1991, it didn't take long for me to return to familiar norms. But our four sons faced some culture shock with southern slang, friendly hellos from strangers, and country music. Throughout life's changes, it is comforting to know that God's Word is our constant. His principles, including authority/submission order, transcend time, place and culture. As for veils, vows or any other sign, Wiersbe states: "The important thing is the submission of the heart to the Lord and the public manifestation of obedience to God's order."[21]

Questions

1. If we reject cultural norms that reflect godly principles, do we attract others to Christianity or repel them?

2. How would you react to a woman wearing a veil in worship today?

3. In your culture, is a man disrespectful if he fails to remove his hat during prayer? Is it a sin or a custom?

4. Roy Deaver wrote: "If the time ever comes when all the impure women of Fort Worth identify themselves by carrying a red purse on their right arm, I will argue strongly – in the light of 1 Cor. 11:2-16 – that it would be a sin for a Christian women of the area to carry a red purse on her right arm" (273). Can one's appearance imply an attitude of insubordination? Why should the Christian avoid such an appearance?

5. Look up 1 Corinthians 11:10 in various translations and see what word is used for "authority."

6. How were the insubordinate angels in Jude 6 and 2 Peter 2:4 punished?

7. Discuss ways in which men and women are mutually dependent.

8. Besides wearing the husband's name and pledging obedience, can you think of any customary symbols of submission today?

9. Everett Ferguson wrote: "The distinction of male and female is an absolute and rests on creation; how that distinction is expressed is culturally relative." Name some ways your culture distinguishes the sexes.

What About
Women's Silence
in the Assembly?

1 Corinthians 14:34-35

Traditions warm our hearts and anchor our souls to friendly experiences from the past. I fondly remember Mama's winter Sunday breakfasts of melt-in-your-mouth orange Danish rolls and steaming hot chocolate. It was a family tradition, just like popcorn balls at Halloween and black-eyed peas on New Year's Day. To me, life wouldn't be the same without them.

Churches have traditions, too. In our assemblies, we stand during the invitation song. Many have a general order of two or three songs, a prayer, and a scripture reading before the sermon. I knew of a congregation that spread a white tablecloth over the communion trays. These practices are traditions. It's not unscriptural to change them, although it might make some people uncomfortable.

Some practices in the church should not be changed. These activities are based on biblical commands or examples. We gather on the first day of the week (Acts 20:7) and partake of the Lord's Supper (1 Corinthians 11:26ff). Before altering any part of our worship, we should ask whether it is tradition or based on Scripture. When asked why the tablecloth covered the trays, a woman replied, "Our grandmothers did it to keep out the flies." Members, now understanding the "why" behind this practice, may eliminate it. Or they may keep it. It's simply tradition.

Some today are asking if exclusive male leadership in church is a tradition. May women lead in prayer, singing or scripture reading in public worship? Some church leaders say, "Yes," still pointing to Galatians 3:28 as they expand roles for women. Others say, "No," citing 1 Corinthians 14:34: "[L]et the women keep silence in the churches" (ASV). Is male leadership a biblical principle or is it tradition? Great confusion exists. But "God is not the author of confusion" (1 Corinthians 14:33 NKJV). His Word explains the "who" and the "why" behind church leadership and helps us correctly separate divine directive from tradition. We will examine two passages on this subject. This chapter will explore women's submissive silence (vv. 34-35). Chapter 7 will examine leadership roles (1 Timothy 2:8-15).

DISORDER IN WORSHIP

"Let the women keep silence in the churches." What prompted Paul to write this message? As we learned in Chapter 4, Paul heard disturbing news about his converts in Corinth. They were behaving like their arrogant culture. The Christians were involved in arguments, fornication, lawsuits and disorderly worship. Paul wrote this letter to deal with their problems and questions. The women either misunderstood or disputed the reality of submission and questioned the necessity of the veil (1 Corinthians 11). Paul reaffirmed God's hierarchical order: God, Christ, man, woman (v. 3). He told them to keep their veils on and let their role as women of God be seen in worship.

Then, in 1 Corinthians 12-14, Paul rebuked the Corinthians' selfish use of spiritual gifts and their disorderly worship. Sandwiched between these rebukes, Paul presents the solution to their problems – sacrificial love (chapter 13). These immature Christians were glorifying themselves, instead of God, in the assembly. The result was chaotic worship. In chapter 14, Paul gives instructions for restoring order. We find his discussion on women's silence in verses 34-35:

> Let your women keep silent in the churches, for they are not permitted to speak; but they are to be submissive, as the law also says. And if they want to learn something, let them ask their own husbands at home; for it is shameful for women to speak in church (NKJV).[1]

As we have seen, the Greek phrases translated "in the churches" and "in church" signified the worship assembly. Paul said it is shameful for a woman to speak in church – the assembly – not in the Lord's body in general, or they would have to be silent all the time. Paul rebukes three disorderly groups in their public worship assembly: (1) those speaking in tongues, (2) those prophesying, and (3) the women.[2] The first two groups were promoting themselves with their spiritual gifts. But, what about the women? Let's examine Paul's instruction.

REGULATIONS CONCERNING SPIRITUAL GIFTS

Paul begins by reminding the Corinthians that spiritual gifts were for edifying, exhorting and comforting (1 Corinthians 14:3, 12). But they were using their gifts selfishly. Paul told them to "grow up" (v. 20). Correcting the tongue-speaker, he wrote, "[L]et him keep silent in church" (v. 28 NKJV). The word for "silent" here means "say nothing."[3] It does not mean absence of sound. Could he sing? Yes. Paul explained, "[I]f there is no interpreter, let him keep silent in church." Without an interpreter, the message could not be understood and therefore edified no one. Speaking in tongues without an interpreter created disorder, and Paul told them – in that case – to be silent. Their silence was regulated. They could speak if an interpreter was present. This command had nothing to do with their singing.

To those with the gift of prophecy, Paul said, "But if anything is revealed to another who sits by, let the first keep silent" (1 Corinthians 14:30 NKJV). When several prophets spoke at the same time, chaos resulted. Therefore, they were told to speak one at a time. Again, the silence was regulated. This did not affect their singing.

Next, Paul directs that "the women keep silence in the churches: it is not permitted unto them to speak" (1 Corinthians 14:34 ASV). He had given regulations for those speaking in tongues and prophesying – when they could speak and when they were to be silent. But what about the women? Everett Ferguson states, "In contrast to these regulations, Paul's prohibition on women speaking is stated absolutely; provision is made only for their silence, not their speaking.[4] The first two groups were told to be silent during certain circumstances. The women were told to be silent, period. The silence commanded to all three groups was to restore order. This had nothing to do with their singing.

All are commanded to sing, "teaching and admonishing one another in psalms and hymns and spiritual songs" (Colossians 3:16b NKJV). There is no disorder in activities in which members participate together. Owen explains that, in the Mishnah, "the rabbis speak of congregations saying a common blessing. In such circumstances, it appears that all who were present participated in a unison recitation of certain prayers similar to what happens when a modern church recites the Lord's Prayer together."[5] Ferguson writes: "Women would join in the congregational 'Amen' accompanying prayer (1 Corinthians 14:16)," and continues:

> The women, therefore, participate in the group activities of the congregation. The principle of joint participation expressed in these verses would cover unison scripture readings, unison prayer (e.g., reciting the 'Lord's prayer' or other set prayer), unison confessions of faith, and other joint vocal expressions.[6]

Ephesians 5:19 allows "speaking to one another in psalms and hymns and spiritual songs" (NKJV). But these Corinthian women were speaking individually and were, therefore, out of order.

OUT OF ORDER

Bauer's *Greek-English Lexicon* defines the word "speak" here (1 Corinthians 14:34), as "speech, to express oneself."[7] Were these women arrogantly judging or challenging the teachers? Were they merely speaking out of turn? Were they innocently asking questions? Or because Paul is rebuking the misuse of spiritual gifts in this chapter, might they have requested in their letter the right to use their spiritual gifts in the assembly?

Let's examine the first scenario. If the women were judging or challenging the teachers, they displayed a disregard for the authority/submission order. Male spiritual leadership is required in worship (1 Timothy 2:12-14). God does not tolerate opposition to His appointed leaders. Miriam is an example. She was a leader among the women of Israel. On one occasion, she and Aaron spoke against Moses, and God rebuked them both (Numbers 12). He punished Miriam with leprosy, but not Aaron. Why? Smith suggests, "One male spiritual leader could challenge another male spiritual leader, even if he were wrong in his criticism; but such a challenge would not be an option for a woman, as it would threaten the greater principle of male spiritual leadership."[8]

But, if the women were judging or challenging teachers, Paul would likely have addressed their attitude and regulated their speech. He did not write, "Let the women stop challenging the leaders, for they are not permitted to challenge the leaders." Instead, he wrote, "[L]et the women keep silence in the churches: for it is not permitted unto them to speak" (1 Corinthians 14:34 ASV).

Let's look at the second scenario. If the women were interrupting or speaking out of turn, wouldn't Paul have told them to keep silent and let another speak as he did the prophets? He did not regulate the women's speech. Instead, he told them that their speaking was "not permitted," and in 1 Corinthians 14:35, he says, "For it is shameful for a woman to speak in church" (RSV).

Paul made it very clear to the Corinthians that a woman speaking (expressing herself individually, apart from the others in the assembly) was not permissible in church. Why not? First Corinthians 14:34b says, "They are not allowed to speak, but [instead] must be in submission" (NIV). This implies that the role of speaking and the role of submission cannot be fulfilled at the same time – in the assembly. This explains why Paul says that even humbly asking questions in church is not acceptable. "If they want to inquire about something, they should ask their own husbands at home; for it is disgraceful for a woman to speak in the church" (v. 35 NIV).

This provokes the question, "Because the word 'husbands' is used, was Paul speaking only to married women?" The context implies Paul meant all women. Look again at 1 Corinthians 14:34. He did not say "Let the women be submissive to their own husbands" as in Ephesians 5: 22, Titus 2:5 and Colossians 3:18. He said, "they are to be submissive" (NKJV). All the women are commanded to respect male spiritual leadership in church. It is demonstrated by silence. In the original Greek, Paul says that it is disgraceful for a woman [not the women] to speak in church (1 Corinthians 14:35 NIV). Ferguson suggests, "[B]y omitting the article before 'woman' Paul seems to be generalizing the prohibition."[9]

But what about the command to "ask their own husbands at home" (1 Corinthians 14:35 NIV)? The Greek word for "wives" is the same word for "women" and the word for "husbands" is the same for "men."[10] Married women in the congregation could ask questions of their own husbands at home. And the unmarried, being in subjection to a father or guardian, could still take Paul's advice and ask "their own men" at home.[11] Paul expected his readers to use common sense. They knew that unmarried women must obey the same laws as the married. Paul would not limit questions to husbands. Any woman could ask her preacher, elder or Bible class teacher after worship. Paul simply meant that women (all women) must be in submissive silence and reserve questions until after the assembly. Ferguson makes an interesting observation, "Even if the statements are not limited to wives and husbands, this submission, of course, is in the assembly, not a general command for women to be subordinate to men."[12] Male spiritual leadership and authority/submission order seem to apply only in the spiritual realms of home and church.

Finally, let's consider the possibility that the Corinthians asked Paul in their letter whether women could use their spiritual gifts in worship. We have already established, in earlier chapters, that women had spiritual gifts, such as the ability to prophesy. If the Corinthians had asked, "May the women use their spiritual gifts in the assembly?" Paul's answer was "Let your women keep silent in the churches, for they are not permitted to speak; but they are to be submissive, as the law also says" (1 Corinthians 14:34 NKJV). Paul ties this submission to law. To what law was Paul referring?

THE LAW

Bauer's *Greek-English Lexicon* defines "the law" here as "the Pentateuch, the work of Moses the lawgiver."[13] The Pentateuch contains the first five books of the Bible written by Moses. It is a unit called the Torah (the law). Christ referred to the "law and the prophets" many times (Matthew 22:36; Luke 16:16). This law includes not only the Law of Moses but also principles established long before God made that covenant with Israel. Submission to male spiritual leadership is one such principle. Paul had reaffirmed its establishment at creation earlier (in the veil discussion, 11:8-9). Here, in 1 Corinthians 14:34, he declares that this submission principle is grounded in "the law." Some versions of the Bible list Genesis 3:16 as a reference here because God formally pronounced this principle to Eve. But some scholars suggest that Paul had Genesis 2 in mind because the command for submission in the assembly includes all women. Cecil May Jr. offers, "Although it is not known what, if any, specific Mosaic law is being referenced, the Old Testament as a whole reinforces the principle of male spiritual leadership."[14] The authority/submission principle applied to Adam and Eve, Abraham and Sarah, and those under the Law of Moses, the judges and the kings. And it continues today.

The Bible gives no examples of women speaking, reading scripture, or leading prayer in a gender-mixed religious assembly. Instead, throughout Scripture, we see godly women modeling recognition of the submission principle until this incident with the Corinthians. By speaking up independently in the assembly, they were violating that principle and were out of order. Perhaps, we could say they were out of the authority/submission order.

SILENCE - A SYMBOL OF SUBMISSION

Everett Ferguson correctly observed, "The [worship] assembly exemplifies the church as the people of God. Hence, there should be a representation of God's appointed order."[15] How is this order represented in church today? Let us consider two worship assemblies and see which shows God's appointed order. In one assembly, the women are participating equally with men: reading scripture, leading prayer serving communion, etc. In the second, the women are voluntarily keeping silent, allowing and encouraging the men to lead. Recognition of the authority/submission order is unmistakable in the second worship assembly! That recognition was Paul's point earlier in the veil issue.

Some might say, "A woman speaking in the assembly is no big deal." Ferguson observes that God has often used "what we might consider insignificant things as signs to remind us of important truths."

God forbade the use of yeast (leavening) during the period of the Passover. That was a sign to His people. Yeast was allowed at other times, but the lack of it at a certain time was a special sign meant to remind God's people of something important. Its lack was so obvious that even the children noticed and were curious. When the children asked, "What does this mean?," they were to be told of the mighty works God had done for the Israelites (Exodus 12).[16]

When our children and visitors ask why the women are silent in our assemblies, we can tell them about God's authority/submission order. Perhaps He commanded woman's silence because it is a clear symbol of submission – in any culture.

In case some would argue, Paul wrote, "If anyone thinks himself to be a prophet or spiritual, let him acknowledge that the things which I write to you are the commandments of the Lord" (1 Corinthians 14:37 NKJV). Yes, there were (and are today) very spiritual women with a great talent to speak and impart God's Word. But Paul makes it clear that the command for silence is from God, based on the submission principle grounded in the law. It is not based in Jewish tradition or in a male-chauvinist attitude. And it was not a new message for Corinth. It had been preached to all the congregations around them.

AS IN ALL THE CHURCHES

Perhaps the immature Corinthians were going against general church practice. Women kept silence in the assemblies of the other congregations. Notice the structure of 1 Corinthians 14:33-34:

> [33]For God is not a God of confusion, but of peace. [33b]*As in all the churches of the saints, [34]let the women keep silence in the churches* for it is not permitted unto them to speak; but let them be in subjection, as also saith the law (ASV).

Before the 1900s, translators made verse 33 a separate sentence: "For God is not a God of confusion, but of peace, as in all the churches of the saints." The KJV and NKJV place it in the preceding paragraph. But the Greek New Testament begins a new paragraph at 33b (as shown in the italicized structure above).[17] Daniel Arichea Jr., in *The Bible Translator*, notes:

Most modern editions and translations take v. 33b with what follows.... Immediately preceding v. 33, Paul had been discussing the problem of order in the worship service, and he ends his appeal for order by his statement in v. 33a: "For God is a God not of disorder but of peace" (NRSV). This summary statement, so it is claimed, is an appropriate conclusion to the discussion on orderliness in the worship service. In view of this it would seem much better to take v. 33b as related to what follows.[18]

Many brotherhood scholars, such as Everett Ferguson and Cecil May Jr., agree.[19]

Perhaps earlier translators felt it awkward to use the word "churches" twice in one sentence. Bauer's *Greek-English Lexicon* explains that the first term "churches" (v. 33b) means "churches of the saints" (congregations) and the second means "church meetings" (v. 34a, assemblies).[20] So, Paul wrote: "As in all the churches [congregations] of the saints, let the women keep silence in the churches [assemblies]" (ASV).

The Corinthians were making their own rules by allowing women to speak in church. Perhaps they felt enlightened and open-minded. Maybe they wanted to be politically correct. Paul rhetorically asked, "Or did the word of God come originally from you? Or was it you only that it reached?" (1 Corinthians 14:36 NKJV). Had God given these Christians a new revelation? Were they independent interpreters of His Word? Of course not!

Paul informed those who still disputed, "But if anyone is ignorant, let him be ignorant" (1 Corinthians 14:38 NKJV). Other versions read: "If he ignores this, he himself will be ignored" (NIV) and "If any one does not recognize this, he is not recognized" (RSV, NASB). Isn't that a sobering thought? Neither God nor sister congregations recognize those who disobey His commands. Wiersbe notes, "Fellowship is based on the Word, and those who willfully reject the Word automatically break the fellowship (1 John 2:18-19)."[21] Women's silence is commanded in the assembly because, as in all the churches, it demonstrates the submission required by God.

SUMMARY

Scripture teaches us that "the women should keep silence in the churches. For they are not permitted to speak ... it is shameful for a woman to speak in church" (1 Corinthians 14:34-35 RSV). A humble, submissive attitude understands this simple command. We pray that our worship will be acceptable in God's sight. But He did not accept unauthorized worship by Cain (Genesis 4:4-7; Hebrews 11:4) or Nadab and Abihu (Leviticus 10:1-2). He punished the angels who rebelled against their prescribed role (2 Peter 2:4; Jude 6). Christian women, let us enter worship with the distinctiveness of womanhood as we were created. Let our worship demonstrate to the unbeliever our recognition of male spiritual leadership as God has decreed – and not that culture dictates our practice.

Can church leaders give a woman permission to speak? Paul said, "It is not permitted." How can men allow her to do something God does not permit? Exclusive male leadership in the assemblies of the Lord's church is not a tradition. It is grounded in the God-ordained authority/submission principle established from the beginning (Genesis 2:18-22; 3:16; 1 Corinthians 11:3, 8-9; 14:33b-35). All activities involving women in the assembly should be viewed in light of this divinely directed headship order. By keeping silent, Christian women do show – in any place, at any time, in any culture – acknowledgment of God's roles for men and women in worship. There should be no confusion. The message was written plainly to the Corinthian Christians in the first century and its relevance continues for us today.

Questions

1. What does the phrase "in church" in 1 Corinthians 14 signify?

2. What regulations did Paul give to those who spoke in tongues? What regulations did he give to those who prophesied? What regulations did he give to a woman who spoke?

3. What is the difference between a woman speaking independently and women singing or reciting with men?

4. Why was Miriam, and not Aaron, punished with leprosy when both spoke against Moses?

5. To what law was Paul referring when he wrote, "as the law also says" (1 Corinthians 14:34)?

6. Do we have any cultural symbol that shows the authority/submission order in our worship? How does silence show it?

7. How did the congregations around Corinth interpret the command for women's silence in the assembly?

8. Should women exercise their speaking gifts in the assembly today? Can church leaders give her permission?

9. What can women do in the assembly?

10. Name several ways in which women can serve God outside the assembly.

What About
Saved in Childbearing?

1 Timothy 2:8-15

On Aug. 11, 1992, we mourned the loss of my sister Donna. It had been nearly a year since she had been diagnosed with leukemia. She was 36. At her funeral, 4-year-old T.C. looked solemnly at the urn that held her ashes and asked, "Who's going to let my mama out of the box?" My brother-in-law answered, "God will."

I remember how thrilled Donna was when T.C. was born. Her husband has done a fine job of raising him, but it saddens us that she was unable to continue the blessed mothering experiences associated with childbearing. Few scriptures address this subject, but an interesting phrase appears in 1 Timothy 2:15. Paul writes, "[S]he will be saved in childbearing" (NKJV). Does this phrase have meaning for women today? Let's find out.

A LETTER FOR CHURCH LEADERS

Our text is part of a letter Paul wrote to the young evangelist, Timothy. This timid young man was struggling with his ministry in Ephesus. False teachers had polluted the teachings of Christ, and church members were confused about proper Christian conduct. Paul wrote to encourage Timothy:

Although I hope to come to you soon, I am writing you these

instructions so that, if I am delayed, you will know how people ought to conduct themselves in God's household, which is the church of the living God, the pillar and foundation of the truth (1 Timothy 3:14-15 NIV).

First Timothy may be called a manual for church leaders. The following is a brief outline:

Chapter 1 – Stopping false teaching
Chapter 2 – Teaching proper conduct for men and women in worship
Chapter 3 – Qualifications of elders and deacons
Chapter 4 – The church leader's responsibility in his personal life and ministry
Chapter 5 – Directions on how to treat erring Christians, needy widows and elders
Chapter 6 – Having the right motives in ministry

This lesson will examine 1 Timothy 2 in which Paul discusses the behavior of men and women in worship – "not merely 'public' worship, but worship wherever and whenever it is offered."[1] At the end of this message, Paul writes, "[S]he will be saved in childbearing" (v. 15 NKJV).

PUBLIC PRAYERS

Paul begins 1 Timothy 2 by emphasizing the fact that Christians should pray for government leaders and for evangelism. In verse 8, he explains who should lead the prayers: "I desire therefore that the men pray in every place, lifting up holy hands, without wrath and disputing" (ASV).

This was not Paul's personal opinion. He asserted his authority as an apostle in 1:1 and 2:7. The Greek word for "men" here means "males," in contrast to females. It is not the generic word for "mankind." "Every place" here means "in every place of meeting."[2] Is Paul talking about the public worship assembly only? Some believe so. But he does not use the phrase "in church" (the assembly) here as he did in the issue of women's silence (1 Corinthians 14). The context is general church life and points to any setting where Christian men and women pray together. Miller, in his paper presented at the Lubbock

Christian University lectureship in October 1991, wrote: "Chapters 2 and 3 deal with some of the specifics of church life ... . 'Ekklasia' is used in its broader, more general sense and is not limited to the public assembly."[3] Cecil May Jr. agrees: "Bible classes, teen devotionals and small group Bible studies are not and are not intended to be the whole church come together. They are not the assembly, but Paul addresses these situations in 1 Timothy 2:8-15."[4] In verse 8, we see that God ensures male spiritual leadership in all gender-mixed worship/church life settings by placing the responsibility of leading prayers on those he has charged with spiritual leadership – the men.

But not just any men. Paul stresses the moral purity required for the men leading these prayers. "Lifting up hands" described the Jewish posture of opening the palms towards heaven (Nehemiah 8:6; Psalm 141:2; Lamentations 3:41; Luke 24:50), but Paul here means the spiritual posture of the praying heart. Dr. J.W. Roberts, in his book *Letters to Timothy*, points out, "The emphasis is on the descriptive 'holy' hands... . Only those of unquestioned integrity are to be put in places of leadership where they will be representing or leading the congregation."[5] Those harboring anger or having unresolved quarrels are prohibited. In public settings, God requires that only blameless, genuinely spiritual men lead the prayers.

This assessment does not imply that women cannot pray or that men act as mediators. All are commanded to "pray, and not to faint" (Luke 18:1 ASV) and to "pray without ceasing" (1 Thessalonians 5:17). In Acts 1:14, we read, "These all continued with one accord in prayer and supplication, with the women and Mary the mother of Jesus, and with His brothers" (NKJV). But God commands a distinction in the leading.

MODEST APPAREL

Paul continues his instructions, now focusing on the women:

> Likewise, I want women to adorn themselves with proper clothing, modestly and discreetly, not with braided hair and gold or pearls or costly garments; but rather by means of good works, as befits women making a claim to godliness (1 Timothy 2:9-10 NASB).

For the men, holy leadership is required. For the women, God commands modesty and good works. Women in the affluent commercial city of Ephesus loved attracting attention with showy dress, expensive jewelry and extravagant hairstyles. James E. Gibbons wrote a poem that humorously describes such preoccupation with costly finery.

Worldly Womanhood
(1 Timothy 2:9-10)

She has her hair put up in tiers,
And from her ears hang chandeliers;
Her lips are painted red as blood –
All badges of her "womanhood."

She drapes herself in clothing tight,
A sexy object to the sight;
All bright, aglitter, and aglow,
She makes herself a "one man" show.

Some women today demonstrate this self-promoting attitude that demands, "Look at me!" Although such attire may be allowed at a costume party or in the bedroom, it is not appropriate for women worshiping God. *The Pulpit Commentary* explains that their appearance "ought not to be showy or conspicuous, calculated either to swell the heart of the wearer with pride, or to attract the eyes of others in forgetfulness of the solemnity of public worship."[6]

Paul says women are to adorn themselves with proper clothing, modestly and discreetly. Let's examine these descriptive terms.

• *Proper.* The KJV, NKJV and ASV translate this Greek word as modest, but the original term means "respectable, appropriate." It is fine to wear work clothes in the yard, but are they appropriate for worship? Is coming into God's presence special? Some say God doesn't care what we wear. But He was very specific about the clothing of the priests in Exodus 28-29. Aaron's turban included a gold plate engraved with the words "Holiness to the Lord" (Exodus 28:36-38 NKJV).

What is considered appropriate clothing may vary with culture. A few decades ago, women would not go out for public gatherings in anything other than a dress and heels. Our apparel is more relaxed today, but perhaps too much for worship. Do we not choose our better outfits for the special occasions of life? The section of the closet where "our best" hangs is where we need to choose our apparel for worship. How does God feel when we dress better for work or school than when we gather for prayer? He does not expect the poor woman to wear what she cannot afford. But those who have good clothing should not intentionally wear what is drab or careless. Our appearance should be "respectable." Charles Crouch wrote:

> Dressing down to the most casual modes of our day does not reflect the degree of reverence required by the rule of worship given by Jesus in John 4:23, 24. Those who insist that we must copy the dress styles of the profane, profligate, sensual, sloven, or of some other sub-culture, to make the disadvantaged feel comfortable in church, are listening to the wrong voices. [7]

As we prepare for worship, let our dress be proper, that is respectable and appropriate.

• *Modestly.* Defining what is appropriate and respectable, Paul says we must dress "modestly" (NASB, RSV). The KJV uses a good, old-fashion term: "shamefacedness" ("having a sense of shame"). A shamefaced woman would be embarrassed to wear the plunging necklines, short shorts and bare midriffs common today. Such immodest clothing is not proper. David Roper offers, "The word 'too' can help indicate what is immodest. Immodest clothing can be too tight, too low, too thin, too revealing, too short, too little, too costly, too ostentatious or too anything that calls attention to oneself in the wrong way." [8]

Men who serve communion find it difficult to avoid the distraction of immodest clothing on women sitting in the pew. God created males to be stimulated by the female body. Immodest clothing can cause even a godly man to lust. When he does, it is sin (Matthew 5:28).

In worship, it is the Lord's attention we want to attract. And He demands modesty. God commanded such from the Israelites offering sacrifices. The robes they wore were open underneath, so God commanded, "Nor shall you go up by steps to My altar, that your nakedness may not be exposed on it" (Exodus 20:26 NKJV). He also clothed Adam and Eve in skins because fig leaves did not cover enough (Genesis 3:7, 21).

• *Discreetly.* Finally, Paul says the Christian woman should dress with "moderation" (NKJV), "discreetly" (NASB), "sensibly" (RSV). We saw two forms of this word in our study of the younger women being "sober" and "discreet" (Titus 2:4-5 KJV). It means "having good sense" or "self-control" – not overdressing or underdressing. The woman dressing sensibly does not waste time or money imitating worldly dress and hairstyles. Others should be able to see, by one's decent, modest and sensible appearance, that her mind is on Christ.

Paul mentions "braided hair and gold or pearls" because this was the hairstyle of indiscreet women who flaunted their wealth. Hendriksen gives this description:

> The braids were fastened by jewelled tortoise-shell combs, or by pins of ivory or silver. Or the pins were of bronze with jewelled heads, the more varied and expensive the better. The pin-heads often consisted of miniature images (an animal, a human hand, an idol, the female figure, etc.). Braids, in those days, often represented fortunes. They were articles of luxury! The Christian woman is warned not to indulge in such extravagance.[9]

Paul condemned an extravagant, showy appearance. Instead, the primary focus should be on developing the inner beauty of the heart. He did not forbid cosmetics, jewelry or braiding the hair, but rebuked excess attention on the external. Peter gives similar advice in 1 Peter 3:3-4:

> Your beauty should not come from outward adornment, such as braided hair and the wearing of gold jewelry and fine clothes. Instead, it should be that of your inner self, the unfading beauty of a gentle and quiet spirit, which is of great worth in God's sight (NIV).

Crouch suggests, "There is a direct relationship between the spirit as God would have it adorned, and the clothing which covers the body; for only through the physical body does the spirit express itself."[10] These instructions are practical for life outside the worship setting. But the worship is Paul's focus here.

GOOD WORKS

The woman of God should be adorned, not with immodest and extravagant attire, "but with good deeds, appropriate for women who profess to worship God (1 Timothy 2:10 NIV). No one is more beautiful to God than a woman arrayed in faithful service through acts of kindness (Matthew 5:16; Ephesians 2:10; Titus 2:14). A good reputation for charitable service is the distinctive mark of a true disciple. Paul says this is proper dress for women who profess reverence for God. When we bow in worship with our brothers and sisters, it should not be with hypocrisy. Merely claiming reverence will not do. God looks, not on outward appearance, but on the heart (1 Samuel 16:7). Proverbs 31:30 tells us that outward show is deceptive and temporary, but "a woman who fears the Lord, she shall be praised" (NKJV). Our works will follow us (Revelation 14:13). Whatever we clothe our soul in for worship here on earth is what we will wear for worship in eternity.

CONDUCT IN THE PRAYER/ TEACHING SETTING

Next, Paul gives instructions for women in church life, specifically teaching/learning situations (Bible study). "Let a woman learn in quietness with all subjection" (1 Timothy 2:11 ASV). This was a new concept for many. Some of the Jewish women had never been allowed to learn Scripture. A quotation in the Palestinian Talmud reads, "Better to burn the Torah than to teach it to a woman."[11] In contrast, the Gentile converts in Ephesus, influenced by female-liberating paganism, may have needed instruction. Women in Asia, like the Roman women, had wealth and rank, engagement in private businesses, service in public offices, and prominent roles in religious cults.[12] Perhaps their tendency to enjoy the spotlight carried over into church gatherings. So Paul explained that the divine authority/submission order requires that they learn in quietness with all submission.

The Greek word for quietness here is not the same as the term for silence in 1 Corinthians 14:34.[13] Bauer's *Greek-English Lexicon* gives the preferred meaning as "settled down, a peaceable disposition," as in 2 Thessalonians 3:12: "Now them that are such we command and exhort in the Lord Jesus Christ, that with quietness they work, and eat their own bread" (ASV). Paul used the same word in 1 Timothy 2:2 when he talked about the importance of praying for government leaders "that we may lead a quiet and peaceable life in all godliness and reverence" (NKJV). This peaceable attitude certainly supports the silence required in the public assembly (1 Corinthians 14) but allows women to speak quietly in other teaching/learning settings.

Some believe that the word for quietness here implies silence.[14] Many are not comfortable with women speaking in Bible class, especially in the auditorium where afterward she must be silent in assembly. Ferguson suggests:

> Although it may be scriptural for a woman to speak in public situations other than the assembly of the church, it may not be expedient. We may compare Paul's discussion of eating meat offered to idols in 1 Corinthians 10 as causing someone to violate his or her conscience. Moreover, it may give the wrong impression to those who do not understand the distinction between "as a church" and other meetings.[15]

If it offends some or if the elders ask the women not to speak in class, the Christian woman should respond "with all subjection." The fellowship and consciences of our brothers and sisters are more important than our need to be heard in class. We are commanded to learn, and we can do that with or without speaking. Separate classes for men and women would also allow women's participation without violating Scripture or conscience if some are offended.

NO AUTHORITY OVER A MAN

Paul says women are to learn – not teach – when men and women gather to study God's Word.

> But I permit not a woman to teach, nor to have dominion over a man, but to be in quietness. For Adam was first formed, then Eve; and Adam was not beguiled, but the woman being beguiled hath fallen into transgression (1 Timothy 2:12-14 ASV).

He does not forbid women teaching the Bible altogether. They may teach younger women (Titus 2:3-5), children (2 Timothy 1:5; 3:15), and individuals in private study. Priscilla and her husband, Aquila, taught Apollos (Acts 18:24-28). But in Bible classes, devotionals, small group studies and other such church life settings, God commands men to fulfill their spiritual leadership responsibility by doing the teaching. Women are to be in quietness.

This brings up a question. May a female Bible class teacher teach young boys after they are baptized? Paul says she may not teach nor have authority over "a man" (*aner* – any adult male).[16] What age might Paul have had in mind to distinguish a boy from a man? Aristophanes of Byzantium, a librarian at Alexandria in the late second century B.C., created a list of age terms cited by scholars well into the middle ages.[17] The last stage of childhood was called *pais* (approximately 7-14 years old). Jesus, at age 12, was still considered a child and was subject to a woman, His mother (Luke 2:42-52). It has been suggested that a man (*aner*) is one who has passed puberty and is able to father a child.[18] Because Scripture does not specify an exact age when a child becomes an adult, God expects us to use common sense. Perhaps local elders may choose an age limit for boys having female teachers. Because baptism does not physically or mentally thrust a boy suddenly into manhood, it appears a woman is not violating Scripture by continuing to teach him after he is baptized. His maturity (or immaturity) should be considered before moving him to an older class.

Another question frequently asked is, "May a woman teach or have authority over men in secular areas, such as business, education or politics?" Ferguson says:

> The instructions in 1 Timothy 2 closely parallel those given in 1 Corinthians 14. Both prohibit women from praying and preaching or teaching in the church's assembly.... Women may teach elsewhere. ... The prohibition of exercising authority over men, therefore, is not a general principle applicable to any situation, but has a specific reference to the assembled church.[19]

Thus, a woman may teach a college English class, serve as a high school principal, act as an administrator over a business, and even govern a country. She is not violating Scripture by teaching or having authority over men outside the spiritual realms of church and home. But in these two areas, she must show recognition of God's authority/submission order (1 Corinthians 11; 1 Timothy 2; Ephesians 5). To do otherwise is to reject male spiritual leadership.

Paul's message was not simply for the first-century church. The basis for gender distinctive roles was given in 1 Corinthians 11:3, 8-9 (creation order and purpose), and 1 Corinthians 14 (the law). In this letter to Timothy, Paul explains women's restriction in teaching, "For Adam was formed first, then Eve. And Adam was not deceived, but the woman being deceived, fell into transgression" (1 Timothy 2:14 NKJV). Hendriksen says:

> Hence, let none of her daughters follow her in reversing the divinely established order. Let none assume the role that was not intended for her. Let not the daughter of Eve teach, rule, lead, when the congregation gathers for worship. Let her learn, not teach; obey, not rule; follow, not lead.[20]

The divine injunction was established in the beginning and has not changed. In the church life setting, Paul says a woman is not to teach, nor to have dominion (authority) over a man. Church leaders who allow her to teach or (in this way)[21] exercise authority over men are allowing her to do something and to have something God does not allow.

SAVED IN CHILDBEARING

God wonderfully (and intentionally) designed woman for suitable helping, not for spiritual headship. Paul reminds us of Eve's wrongful attempt to lead. "And Adam was not deceived, but the woman being deceived, fell into transgression" (1 Timothy 2:14 NKJV). But that does not endanger salvation for women. Paul continues, "[B]ut she shall be saved through her child-bearing, if they continue in faith and love and sanctification with sobriety" (v. 15 ASV). The singular pronoun "she" and plural pronoun "they" may seem confusing. Guy N. Woods offers an explanation:

> Thus, the meaning would appear to be: Eve, representative of womankind, was deceived in the transgression and because of this her sex bears restrictions in teaching; this, however, will not keep women from being saved provided they practice the precepts of faith, love and sobriety, i.e., live the Christian life![22]

What does Paul mean by "saved through her child-bearing"? Let us see what he is not saying. He is not saying Christian women are promised literal and universal safety in the dangerous process of delivering children. We know that many godly women have died bringing babies into the world. He is not saying that only women who bear children (and/or raise them in the Lord) can go to heaven. Paul is talking about women in general.

This statement appears at the end of a discussion on the distinctive roles of men and women. Paul had stated that, in worship/church life settings, women are to learn in quietness and are not to teach or have authority over men. Lest this restriction discourage some, Paul offers encouragement. Yes, a woman prompted the first sin, but she was not dismissed from God's plan for mankind. But she (woman in general) will find salvation in childbearing. God created within her body the organs that house and nourish children; thus, the word "childbearing" sums up her role as wife, mother, and maintainer of the home. She has the capacity to bear children, but it is not a requirement. Although all do not marry or have children, women (as a whole) receive God's blessing of salvation, not by seeking man's place, but by keeping her own.[23]

God has created a special sphere for woman – a realm in which she, and not man, was designed to serve the Lord and influence the world. Hendriksen writes, "It is his will that the woman should influence mankind 'from the bottom up' (that is, by way of the child), not 'from the top down' (that is, not by way of the man)."[24] Although male spiritual leadership is God's plan, Ferguson asserts:

> This of course does not mean that women do not have the capacity to fill the public leadership role in the church; they may do it as well or better than men. That is not the question. As there is a function reserved for women, so there is a function that God for some reason has chosen to reserve for men. Salvation comes from respecting these distinct female and male roles."[25]

Simply remaining in their God-given role does not guarantee salvation to women. They must "continue in faith, love, and holiness, with self-control" (1 Timothy 2:15 ETR). Women who do not continue in these attitudes cannot expect salvation.

God has a place for us as women. It is not in spiritual leadership over men. Let us not be deceived like Eve. Our focus should be not on our restriction (in the home or church) but on our gifts – especially the blessings of personal relationship with God, our hope of salvation, and our uniquely female privilege of childbearing!

Questions

1. Why does God command men to lead the prayers in every place?

2. What would prohibit a man from leading prayers?

3. Concerning women's dress, what does the term "proper" mean?

4. What does the term "shamefacedness" mean?

5. What problems can immodest clothing cause in worship?

6. What did "braided hair and gold or pearls" mean in the Ephesian culture (1 Timothy 2:9)?

7. What is the meaning of the phrase "learn in quietness" (1 Timothy 2:11 ASV)?

8. Under what circumstances are women prohibited from teaching? Why?

9. How can women influence the world through childbearing?

10. How can women influence the world without childbearing?

What About
The Widow Indeed?

1 Timothy 5:1-10

My mother-in-law, Peggy Guy, attends a ladies Bible class taught by former Catholic nun Joanne Howe at the Hendersonville, Tenn., Church of Christ. Howe's book *A Change of Habit* describes her early desire to give her life to God.[1] She talks about her years of training and teaching in various convents, her dissatisfaction with Catholicism, and her conversion to the Lord's church. Her inspiring story shows the perspective of those so devoted to God that they pledge themselves to celibacy and dedicate their lives to good works in His service.

Did you know a similar group of women was in the early church? It was made up of elderly widows who made a special agreement not to remarry and to give full attention to the Lord's work. In return, they were financially supported by the local congregation. These women did not occupy an office as elders do, but they were set apart for special duties. *The International Standard Bible Encyclopedia* says that their special duties included "praying and fasting, visiting the sick, instruction of women, preparing them for baptism, assisting in the administration of this sacrament."[2] Because of social barriers between men and women in the first century, this group of widows was an effective resource for the church.

We read about this group of widows in Paul's manual for church leaders (1 Timothy). In Chapter 7, we were introduced to Paul's letter that encouraged Timothy to confront false teachers, safeguard proper worship, and develop leaders in the church. We saw its general outline on page 72. This lesson will cover Paul's instructions in 1 Timothy 5 for rebuking erring Christians, including women, and for dealing with needy widows.

REPRIMANDING CHRISTIANS

First, Paul tells Timothy to correct Christians gently as members of his own family (1 Timothy 5:1-2). To the aged man, he should show respect, not rebuking harshly, but admonishing (begging, persuading) as he would his own father. Leviticus 19:32 commands such an attitude of respect: "You shall rise before the gray headed and honor the presence of an old man, and fear your God: I am the Lord" (NKJV). Paul then explains that an erring younger man should also be treated with kindness, as a brother.

When it is necessary to correct an older woman, she must be treated with courtesy, as one's own mother – lovingly and with deep humility. When reprimanding a young woman, the church leader must speak to her as a sister, kindly and respectfully "with all purity." He must avoid suspicion in his teaching relationship. My husband urges his ministry students never to counsel or study with a woman alone. If David, a man after God's own heart, succumbed to lust with Bathsheba, young men today should not think themselves invulnerable to temptation. Barnes suggests, "A youthful minister who fails here, can never recover the perfect purity of an unsullied reputation, and never in subsequent life be wholly free from suspicion."[3]

CARE OF WIDOWS

Next, Paul discusses the charitable treatment of widows (1 Timothy 5:3-16). He identifies five types:
• The worthy widow who has no means of support (the widow indeed);
• The widow who has family to support her;
• The unworthy widow who should not be supported by the church;
• The supported "enrolled" (v. 9 ASV) widow who serves the church;
• The young widow who should not be enrolled as a supported worker.

• *A Widow Indeed (1 Timothy 5:3)*
Widows have a special place in God's heart (Deuteronomy 14:29; Psalms 68:5; 94:6; Malachi 3:5). Paul writes, "Honor widows that are widows indeed" (1 Timothy 5:3 KJV). The word for honor in this context means to "support or provide financially for." Of course, supporting all widows would overburden the church, so Paul limits assistance to certain widows (in the church, Galatians 6:10). The word "widow" comes from a word meaning "to lack or be deprived." She has been deprived of her husband. If she has no means of financial support and no children to provide for her, she is indeed deprived, and is "really a widow" (v. 5 NKJV). Care for such destitute widows may come from the alms of the faithful as *The Pulpit Commentary* beautifully explains:

> Let them have a special place in reverent care and common prayer, as they have a lot which is so isolated and so hard – a battle so keen and terrible, and as they find that the slender means are so soon spent. The lonely hours are full of pictures of the past: as wives they were the first to be thought of and provided for – the best was for them, the first place at the table and in the heart was theirs; so honour them, for they are sensitive to slight and indifference. Let the Church counteract the neglect of the world.[4]

Paul describes a qualification and a job for this widow. "Now she who is really a widow, and left alone, trusts in God and continues in supplications and prayers night and day" (1 Timothy 5:5 NKJV). This widow is alone and perhaps too old or feeble to work. Without even family to help, she indeed has no one on whom she can depend – except God. She truly believes He is her "refuge and strength, A very present help in trouble" (Psalm 46:1 NKJV). She trusts (hopes in, expects) Him to care for her now as He always has. Her devotion is real and visible – not in occasional prayers offered only in emergencies – but in continual vigils "night and day." *The Pulpit Commentary* describes her prayer life.

> Did she not in the dark hours fling her arms around her Father's neck; did she not tell him that she would fear no want, though she felt such change? Did not that trust – sim-

ple trust – do her more good than all human words, all kindly letters, all change of place and scene?

She reveals [prayer's] power by her perseverance in it … . She whose tears have watered her couch, whose hand has reached forth into the empty space, whose every movement would once have awakened solicitude, as of pain, or weariness, or sleeplessness, is now alone. But not alone."[5]

Anna was an example of such a devoted widow. This 86-year-old woman "did not depart from the temple, but served God with fastings and prayers night and day" (Luke 2:37 NKJV). Although these righteous widows were frail in body, their continual supplications to God on behalf of the church created a mighty force for good (James 5:16). Such devoted prayer warriors must have been a real asset to the congregation.

• *The Widow With Family (1 Timothy 5:4)*

"But if any widow has children or grandchildren, let them first learn to show piety at home and to repay their parents; for this is good and acceptable before God" (1 Timothy 5:4 NKJV). This is welfare as God intended it.[6] Children and grandchildren of widows should provide for their needs. The word translated "nephew" in the KJV originally meant any descendants sprung from or born of her direct line.[7] God commands her offspring to repay the debt (so to speak) for her unselfish care when they were young. Parents and grandparents generally do the giving, and children generally take from their hands. Therefore, these descendants need "to learn" (discover by experience) to practice the religious convictions they profess.

Paul explains that a person must provide for his own kinfolk, and especially for his own household (immediate family). The word "provide" means to "to see in advance." We all know the day may come when our own parents will need support. Special friends of ours, Frank and Beverly Bradford of Henderson, Tenn., built a small house next to their own, anticipating their parents' needs. When Frank's mother passed away in 2000, his father moved into the cottage. Such providing pleases God (1 Timothy 5:4). Of course, not all elderly parents want to live with their children. And not all children are able to take in elderly parents. But God's command can be obeyed if young adults will see needs in advance. Planning ahead, with family discussion, will help avoid conflict and guilt feelings. Ephesians 6:1-3 tells us to honor our father and mother. We never outgrow this command. Jesus condemned the practice of "corban," a gift to the temple that excused one from supporting his parents (Matthew 15:4-6). Remember that Jesus, Himself, made provision for His mother as He hung on the cross (John 19:26-27). Such obligation was common knowledge. In ancient Greek law, a citizen was legally bound to care for his parents. One who failed to do so lost his civil rights. Philo, an ancient philosopher, used an example from nature: "When old storks become unable to fly, they remain in their nests and are fed by their children, who go to endless exertions to provide their food because of their piety."[8]

Paul wrote, "But if anyone does not provide for his own, and especially for those of his household, he has denied the faith and is worse than an unbeliever" (1 Timothy 5:8 NKJV). If the heathen care for their parents, what might unbelievers think of Christians who shirk their obligations in this matter? Christian adults who burden the church instead of providing for their loved ones give fuel to those who would sneer at our religion.

Sacrificial (*agape*) love for our widowed mother or grandmother may involve financial support in a nursing home or assisted living facility. But these places can be very lonely. We cannot assume God is pleased with mere physical care. *Phileo* love (affection and feeling of emotion) is required for our husbands and children (Titus 2:4). Should our parents receive less? Barclay suggests that providing for our own "is repaying love received in time of need with love given in time of need; and only with love can love be repaid."[9]

• *The Unworthy Widow (1 Timothy 5:6)*
Some widows are not worthy of financial support from the church because they are not devoted to God. Paul describes such a widow: "But she who lives in pleasure is dead while she lives" (1 Timothy 5:6 NKJV). Some women, after losing their husbands, seek sensual and material pleasures. Although physically alive, they are dead to the more important spiritual interests. *The Pulpit Commentary* illustrates:

There is no movement of thought towards God; no feet swift to do his will; no heart that beats in sympathy with his Law. Instinct is alive; but the brightness of the eye, and the music of the voice, and the activities of life, are like flowers upon graves.[10]

Such self-indulgent and unspiritual women on the church payroll would hurt its reputation rather than represent its true nature to the world. Wiersbe writes:

> It has been my experience ... that godly widows are "spiritual powerhouses" in the church. They are the backbone of the prayer meetings. They give themselves to visitation, and they swell the ranks of teachers in the Sunday School. It has also been my experience that, if a widow is not godly, she can be a great problem to the church. She will demand attention, complain about what the younger people do, and often "hang on the telephone" and gossip.[11]

Paul's audience needed to understand and practice these instructions. The church's reputation was at stake. He wrote, "Give the people these instructions, too, so that no one may be open to blame (1 Timothy 5:7 NIV). Godly people take care of their own. Such care attracts others to the gospel. But a professed believer who neglects his aged parents is worse than an infidel, and an unspiritual widow sponging off the church gives cause for ridicule.

• *The "Enrolled" Widow (1 Timothy 5:9)*

The *Apostolic Church Order*, written about A.D. 300, distinguished two groups of widows supported by the church: "one for prayer [perhaps those too old or frail for work] and the other for service to women in illness or need."[12] First Timothy 5:9-10 lists qualifications for widows who may be "enrolled" (ASV, RSV), "put on the list" (NIV, NASB), "taken into the number" (KJV). Paul employed a classical Greek word here used for enlisting soldiers. *The Apostolic Tradition*, attributed to Hippolytus (about A.D. 215), says that "when a widow is appointed, she is not ordained but she shall be chosen by name."[13] Paul gives qualifications for widows who could be appointed.

Do not let a widow under sixty years old be taken into the
number, and not unless she has been the wife of one man,
well reported for good works: if she has brought up children, if she has lodged strangers, if she has washed the saints'
feet, if she has relieved the afflicted, if she has diligently
followed every good work (1 Timothy 5:9-10 NKJV).

(1) She must be at least 60 years old. Mature women would be less
likely to desire remarriage and more likely to remain committed to
God's service. The ancient world considered 60 "specially suited for
concentration on the spiritual life."[14]

(2) She must have been the wife of one man. Having one spouse is
also a qualification for elders (1 Timothy 3:2; Titus 1:6) and deacons
(1 Timothy 3:12). Some suggest that she could have been married only
once. Anna is described as a widow "of a great age, and had lived with
a husband seven years from her virginity; And she was a widow of
about fourscore and four years" (Luke 2:36-37 KJV). But others believe,
as Wiersbe states: "Since younger women were advised to remarry
(5:14), this stipulation cannot refer to a woman who had a temporary
second marriage after the death of her husband."[15] Roberts suggests
that she must not have been put away or divorced either for a scriptural or unscriptural reason."[16] Fidelity is the important quality here.

(3) She must be well-reported for good works. Paul had mentioned
such good works in his discussion of proper Christian conduct (1 Timothy
2:10). Matthew 5:16 says we must let our light shine and glorify God
by our good works. Paul lists the good works in which this godly woman
must have participated.

She has brought up children. A woman experienced in raising children would be qualified to care for orphans and teach younger women
how to be good mothers. It was not necessary that she had physically
borne babies. Some women raised children who were abandoned in a
common pagan practice called "exposure":

When a child was born, it was brought and laid before the
father's feet. If the father stooped and lifted the child, that
meant that he acknowledged it and was prepared to accept
responsibility for its upbringing. If the father turned and

walked away, then the child was quite literally thrown out, like an unwanted piece of rubbish.[17]

Some exposed children were picked up and raised as prostitutes, slaves and gladiators. But those rescued by godly women were blessed. **She must have practiced hospitality.** In Paul's day, lodging was scarce, expensive and often dirty and unsafe. Ferguson suggests that, as an enrolled widow, she "could be maintained in her own house to provide a guest house to receive traveling Christians, very necessary in an age without many adequate accommodations for travelers."[18] We find examples of hospitality in the Old Testament in the widow of Zarephath, who refreshed Elijah (1 Kings 17:9) and the Shunammite woman, who prepared a guest room for Elisha (2 Kings 4:8-11). **She must be one who has washed the saints' feet.** This does not refer to a religious act. Washing feet was a sign of hospitality to guests because sandals gave little protection from dust and mud. Washing dirty feet is a sign of humility as Jesus taught His disciples in the upper room (John 13:3-20). The worthy widow must have displayed this quality.

She must have been a reliever of the afflicted. A woman who has shared the burdens of others will continue to be active on the church's behalf by caring for the sick, needy, hungry, sorrowing, persecuted and oppressed. Tertullian wrote in A.D. 204 that their practical experience enabled them to assist others with counsel and comfort.

She must be a follower of every good work. Whenever an opportunity arose, she participated to the best of her ability. She did not whine, "I don't have time" or "That's not my thing." She served with her time, energy, finances and prayers. Her attitude and experience made her a deeply respected and valuable asset.

SUMMARY

The first-century church cared for its widows. One group of destitute widows without family received support and reciprocated with continual prayers for the church. Others over 60, having been the wife of one man, and having participated in good works were sustained to serve in various other ways.

Scripture does not present details on how the program worked. But first-century Christians understood it. Social barriers may have contributed to the need for special female servants to minister to women. They had no government agencies such as we have to care for the aged. The church has not continued the practice of widow enrollment. Only godly widows were chosen for support. The ungodly were excluded because they would bring reproach upon the Lord's family. In Chapter 9, we will discuss another group who were not allowed to be enrolled – the younger widows. We will examine Paul's justification for their exclusion and his directive that they marry "in the Lord."

Questions

1. How should church leaders rebuke older women? What about the younger women?

2. What five types of widows are identified in 1 Timothy 5?

3. Who is the widow "indeed"?

4. Why do children need to learn to take care of their parents and grandparents?

5. What was the penalty in ancient Greek law for those who failed to provide for their parents?

6. Why should the unworthy widow not be supported by the church?

7. According to *The Apostolic Tradition,* "when a widow is appointed, she is not _____ but she shall be chosen by _____."

8. What three main qualifications are required for putting a widow on the list?

9. Does Scripture teach that the enrolled widow program is binding today?

10. Does Scripture teach that the enrolled widow program may be implemented today?

What About
The Younger Widow?

1 Timothy 5:11-16; 1 Corinthians 7:39

In Chapter 8, we began a study of Paul's instructions about the charitable treatment of widows. Five types were identified: the worthy widow who has no other means of support (the widow indeed); the widow who has family to support her; the unworthy widow who should not be supported by the church; the supported "enrolled" widow who serves the church; and the young widow who should not be "enrolled" as a supported worker. Having discussed the first four groups, let us now explore Paul's message for the younger widow.

REFUSE THE YOUNGER WIDOW

Who is considered the younger widow? She is under the age of 60 and, therefore, not old enough to be put on the list of enrolled widows. Paul writes: "As for younger widows, do not put them on such a list. For when their sensual desires overcome their dedication to Christ, they want to marry" (1 Timothy 5:11 NIV). This verse explains why younger widows were refused. Apparently, an enrolled widow took a pledge, or at least an agreement, not to remarry. She made a commitment to dedicate her life in service to the church. Wiersbe comments:

> The pledge Paul referred to was probably a more or less formal commitment, taken on joining the list of widows, where-

in the woman vowed to serve Christ entirely without thought of remarriage. In this way she could devote herself without distraction to the Lord (1 Corinthians 7:34-35).[1]

Her life became her work of ministering to the sick, orphans, travelers and the needs of other women. But after pledging her full attention to the Lord's service, the younger widow might begin to struggle between her physical desires and her spiritual commitment. A life of prayer and ministry might prove too restraining for her. She would naturally be attracted to men. Paul did not condemn her for these natural desires, nor did he prohibit remarriage. In fact, in 1 Timothy 5:14, he urges her to remarry.

He knew that if younger women were enrolled, some would rebel and "grow wanton against" (1 Timothy 5:11 NKJV) the work of Christ. The word "wanton" meant "drawn away by one's own sensuous impulses." The NIV says, "For when their sensual desires overcome their dedication to Christ, they want to marry." Hendricksen notes: "[T]he importance of the work required whole-hearted devotion. If the interests are divided, so that the widow's mind, even during the performance of her spiritual functions, is pre-occupied with the idea of finding a suitable husband, her efficiency will suffer."[2]

A lack of efficiency was not the only problem Paul had in mind. Enrolled widows who ended their ministry to remarry broke a solemn vow and tarnished their reputation and Christian influence. First Timothy 5:12 says they have "cast off" (NKJV), "broken" (NIV), "set aside" (NASB), "violated" (RSV) their first faith. "Faith" here meant promise or pledge. By breaking this pledge, they have "condemnation" (NKJV) or "bring judgment on themselves" (NIV). Vows (pledges) have always been a serious matter in God's eyes. In the laws given to Moses, if a woman made a vow and her husband voided it, it was annulled. But the widow who had no husband to void hers was expected to keep her pledge.

> Also any vow of a widow or a divorced woman, by which she has bound herself, shall stand against her. If she vowed in her husband's house, or bound herself by an agreement with an oath, and her husband heard it, and made no response to her and did not overrule her, then all her vows

shall stand, and every agreement by which she bound herself shall stand (Numbers 30:9-11 NKJV).

A broken vow incurred judgment. Paul did not mean the young widow was condemned to hell. But she brought reproach upon herself and the church. Her witness to unbelievers was destroyed if she became enrolled, declared a strong faith, renounced worldly pleasures, relied wholly on God by accepting support from the church – and then changed her mind. Paul may have considered the words of Jesus in Luke 9:62: "No one who puts his hand to the plow and looks back is fit for service in the kingdom of heaven" (NIV). He wanted to protect the young widow from this guilt and judgment. Therefore, he said the church should not allow her to make the commitment of the widow's life of prayer and service.

THEY LEARN TO BE IDLE

Paul gives another reason not to place young widows on the list. "And besides, they learn to be idle, wandering about from house to house" (1 Timothy 5:13 NKJV). No longer having a husband to do things for, the young widow might learn or "get into the habit of" (NIV) idleness. Unlike the aged woman, the younger has not matured into a stable and dependable work ethic. The old saying is true: "Idleness is the devil's workshop." Paul wrote to the Thessalonians, "We hear that some among you are idle. They are not busy; they are busybodies" (2 Thessalonians 3:11 NIV).

Women, in general, love interpersonal relationship. If we spend time alone or with small children, we crave adult conversation. There was a real possibility that these young women would become not only idle but also gossips (tattlers, ASV) and busybodies, "saying things which they ought not" (1 Timothy 5:13 NKJV). As they carried out their visitation and ministry assignments from house to house, they might stir up excitement by telling the secrets or personal business of one neighbor to another. The Lord prefers younger women to follow the path of the virtuous one in Proverbs 31:27, "She watches over the affairs of her household and does not eat the bread of idleness" (NIV).

MARRY AND BEAR CHILDREN

If the needy younger widow could not be enrolled, what should she do? Paul writes, "Therefore I desire that the younger widows marry, bear children, manage the house, give no opportunity to the adversary to speak reproachfully" (1 Timothy 5:14 NKJV). By inspiration, he recommends that a young widow marry and fill her life with the activities for which she was designed: having children and making a home. Little girls imagine themselves happily married and rocking their babies. God never intended young women (or men) to live in celibacy, although Paul encouraged it during times of persecution (1 Corinthians 7). First Timothy 4:1-3 states that religions forbidding marriage teach a false doctrine.

Paul does not command these younger widows to marry but suggests it is better for them than to be idle and to fall into mischief. He wanted happiness for young widows and knew that they were more likely to find it in marriage and motherhood than in restrictive prayer and service with the older women. Besides, by remarrying, they could serve the Lord in a way that would help, not burden, the church.

What does Paul mean by "manage the house" (1 Timothy 5:14 NKJV)? The original term is from two words meaning "house" and "manager, ruler or guide." The job may be compared to the manager of a sports team. Hands-on participation (being a home-worker) is necessary (Titus 2:4). But Mom is not required to do all the work herself. She is responsible for making sure it gets done. She must train her family to do their part and teach them that if anyone fails to do their job, everyone suffers – just as a sports team. Sandra Felton, on a 2004 *Focus on the Family* radio program, told the story of a mother who noticed one of her children did not set the table for dinner one night. She did not rebuke the child; she simply called everyone to dinner and began passing the food. The other children, knowing who dropped the ball, hurriedly moved the slacker to action.

Managing the home is not easy. The day shift is not completed in eight hours. The pay cannot be measured in dollars. But, "Who can find a virtuous wife? For her worth is far above rubies" (Proverbs 31:10 NKJV). No monetary value equals a woman who manages a peaceful, godly home. "Her children rise up and call her blessed; Her husband also, and he praises her: 'Many daughters have done well, But you excel them all' " (vv. 28-29 NKJV).

A woman's life can be divided roughly into three periods. Her first 20 years might be spent developing herself spiritually, physically, intellectually and socially to be the best she can be. Her next 20-year period is the joyful, yet strenuous, time to raise children – passing on her spiritual and earthly legacy. In her last 20 years, she has the chance to give back, to "lay sticks on the fire" built by others, in her school, church and community. All three periods have rewards. But the greatest comes to mothers who create spiritually healthy homes and raise their children in the Lord: "I have no greater joy than to hear that my children walk in truth" (3 John 4 NKJV). Isaiah 54:13 says, "And all your sons will be taught of the Lord; And the well-being of your sons will be great" (NASB). Mine are. My son Nathan is ministering in England, and I have no greater joy. My other three sons are faithful Christian men of God in other areas.

God designed woman, physically and emotionally, for a ministry of managing the home. Circumstances may necessitate the househusband, but this is not his appointed duty. Paul's words here support God's blueprint for the home. When a woman is responsible in marriage, parenting and homemaking, she gives the "enemy" (NIV, "adversary," KJV) no occasion to speak against Christianity (1 Timothy 5:14; Titus 2:5). In other words, if the marriage is healthy, the home peaceful, and the children disciplined and godly, others can see that God's Word is true. And they are attracted to the gospel.

Paul concludes his discussion on the younger widows in verse 15 of 1 Timothy: "For some have already turned aside after Satan" (NKJV). This suggests that some younger women had already been added to the list of enrolled widows and had found that restrictive life too difficult. Paul wanted to avoid this possibility with other younger widows.

INDIVIDUAL RESPONSIBILITY

The instructions about widows ends with 1 Timothy 5:16: "If any woman who is a believer has widows in her family, she should help them and not let the church be burdened with them, so that the church can help those widows who are really in need" (1 Timothy 5:16 NIV). The KJV says, "If any man or woman believeth," but later Greek manuscripts

(Nestles and United Bible Society) do not include the words "man or." Paul seems to be instructing widows (or single women) who are financially able to care for other needy widows. Hendricksen explains:

> Here, let us say, is a lady like Lydia, who has a spacious home. She has a servant, a friend, or a relative, who happens to be a widow. Perhaps she can provide a home for that widow, or even for more than one widow. Or else she can help the widow financially or by providing work. Let her then do her Christian duty so that God may be glorified, so that this gracious lady may herself experience in her heart the peace which results from divine approval of deeds well done, and so that the needy one may be relieved.[3]

Christians who provide for the needs of elderly widows relieve the church. They also obey God's command in James 1:27: "Pure and undefiled religion before God and the Father is this: to visit orphans and widows in their trouble" (NKJV). "To visit" means more than simply stopping by to say hello. It implies taking care of needs. Many congregations have programs in which individuals participate in the care of widows. Many churches have a helping hands ministry that divides the names of widows among individuals. If a widow needs a light bulb changed, a ride to the doctor or grocery store, or simply someone to talk to, she knows whom to call. The ministry maintains a list of church members who specialize in automobile repair, carpentry, electrical wiring, etc., to help the widow save money.

Anyone can make opportunities to help the widow. June Wesley, in her article "A Lonely Widow," suggests some kind and helpful things to do:[4]

• Bring food when she is sick.
• Send flowers for her birthday, Christmas and New Year's.
• Send notes of encouragement.
• Come by to take her places with them.
• Pray with her at home or on the phone.
• Talk with her on the phone – or just listen.
• Send magazine subscriptions.
• Take her to lunch, for coffee or for dessert.

• Give or loan her books or tapes.
• Take her to the doctor.
• Help with upkeep around the house.
• Help with hospital bills.

Paul's words concerning widows are helpful for us today although the enrolled widow program does not seem to be binding. Every congregation has worthy widows who may struggle financially. Some churches sponsor nursing homes or assisted living centers. We must not forget that godly widows can still be an excellent spiritual resource.

MARRY "ONLY IN THE LORD"

Paul encouraged younger widows to remarry. In 1 Corinthians 7:39, he says any Christian widow may marry whom she wishes but "only in the Lord." Does this mean she must marry only a Christian?

Remembering the context of 1 Corinthians, we know Paul wrote that letter to deal with church problems and to answer questions. In chapter 7, he discusses sexual relations in marriage (vv. 1-6), celibacy (vv. 5-9), marriage between a Christian and a non-Christian (vv. 10-16), marriage during the "present distress" of persecution (vv. 25-38), and remarriage of widows (vv. 39-40).

At that time, Christians were being persecuted. A normal family life was difficult because at any time a husband or wife may be taken to prison and/or killed for their faith. Therefore, Paul recommended that during that present distress, it was best not to marry: "But I say to the unmarried and to the widows: It is good for them if they remain even as I am [single]" (1 Corinthians 7:8 NKJV). But, he adds, if they lack self-control, it is better for them to marry than to burn with sexual passion (v. 9).

The Corinthians may have asked, in their letter, whether a Christian should stay married to an unbelieving spouse. Perhaps some were being harassed for their faith, or some unbelieving spouses were leaving because of their mate's new religion. Paul replies that the Christian spouse should not leave (1 Corinthians 7:10-16). God has sanctified (set apart) that unbelieving spouse and their children as part of a Christian home. "But," he writes, "if the unbeliever departs, let him depart; a brother or a sister is not under bondage in such cases: but God has called us to peace" (v. 15 NKJV). The Christian spouse should not leave because eventually the unbeliever may be converted (v. 16). In verses 17-24, Paul discusses remaining in the same state in which one was converted, for this does not affect one's relationship with God. The threat of persecution became the focus of his instructions in 1 Corinthians 7:25-38. It is better to be single during such uncertain circumstances. Then, in verse 39, Paul addresses remarriage of the widow. "A wife is bound by law as long as her husband lives; but if her husband dies, she is at liberty to be married to whom she wishes, only in the Lord" (NKJV). Commentators do not all share the same interpretation of "only in the Lord." Many believe she may only marry another Christian. Authors of the *Bible Knowledge Commentary* write:

> The only constraint Paul placed on a widow who sought remarriage was the obligation to marry another Christian (he must belong to the Lord) – an obligation which though previously unstated, he no doubt meant to apply to all who sought marriage partners.[5]

Coffman agrees, citing Paul's words in his second Corinthian letter, "Be ye not unequally yoked together" (6:14 (KJV).

> Yes, widows might indeed marry again, but "only in the Lord." It was never intended that Christians marry unbelievers, as Paul spelled out more fully in 2 Corinthians 6:14ff. It is a rare and exceptional thing indeed that mixed marriages between Christians and unbelievers can produce anything but sorrow.[6]

David Lipscomb also held that view. He believed 2 Corinthians 6:14-18 taught that Christians should "be not unequally yoked together" anytime the believer could be controlled by the unbeliever. He wrote that, in the Law of Moses, God's people could not marry out of the family of Israel lest they be pulled away from God, adding, "[T]he spirit and teaching of the Bible is against Christians marrying those not members of the body of Christ, and yet there is no direct and specific prohibition of it, other than for widows." [7]

Some agree that Paul might be commanding widows to marry only Christians but that "in the Lord" means "with God's approval." Jim McGuiggan argues that "be not unequally yoked" does not apply to marriage, mentioning our inconsistency in following the rest of the message in 2 Corinthians 6:

> The widow is permitted to remarry …. She may marry whom she will. But she is to do it "in the Lord." As the Lord approves, allows, bearing in mind in whom she lives and moves (see Ephesians 6:1; 1 Corinthians 11:11). Moffatt says she must marry a Christian. Perhaps he's right. I can understand that position being taken. I can also understand 2 Corinthians 6:14ff being used to oppose marriages between saints and the unforgiven. What I can't understand is our not insisting on breaking these marriages up since 2 Corinthians 6:17 says: 'Come out from among them; be ye separate.' They broke them up in Ezra 10.[8]

James Meadows, in his article "The Widow and 'In the Lord,' " asks more questions about the application of this phrase. He presents others' views that (1) "only in the Lord" is not an adjective modifying the man the widow is marrying, but an adverb indicating the manner in which the action is done, and (2) that the widow may marry whom she pleases if she remains a faithful Christian and does not violate scripture.[9]

R.C.H. Lenski comments on both interpretations:

> "Only in the Lord" would be beyond question if the Christian widow be married to a Christian husband. Paul seems to have that in mind in this "judgment" (v. 25) which he is delivering to the Corinthians. Yet many take "only in the Lord" in a wider sense, namely, "in a Christian way" or "in the fear of the Lord," asking his blessing. For there are causes in which a marriage with a non-Christian may be justified.[10]

What can we conclude about the widow's remarriage? Many of these Corinthians had mates who were not converted. We have mentioned that perhaps some were being harassed for their faith or their unbelieving spouses had left. But it is also possible that Paul had stressed the importance of marriage between Christians and they were asking in their letter whether Christians should come out of marriages to unbelievers. Paul's reply was, "No." The law of marriage was established in the beginning (Matthew 19), just as the authority/submission principle was, and Christianity did not dissolve it.

To their question, "What about the widow?" Paul answered that "if her husband dies, she is at liberty to be married to whom she wishes, only in the Lord" (1 Corinthians 7:39 NKJV). It appears Paul meant that a widow must marry a Christian. Lipscomb is right in that the spirit and teaching of Scripture is that Christians should marry Christians.

Is it a sin to marry an unbeliever? Meadows offers, "Certainly it is dangerous and, in most cases, highly inexpedient for a Christian to marry a non-Christian, but to say that a thing is dangerous is one thing, and to say that it is a sin is something else."[11] If a religiously mixed marriage is sinful, Paul would not have told the new converts to remain with their unbelieving spouse.

Many today are married to unbelievers. They should remain in the marriage. This also applies to the former widow. Not having understood the wiser course, she should now strive to convert that mate. Chapter 10 will explain the biblical formula for converting the unbelieving husband (1 Peter 3:1-2).

While we were growing up, my mother stressed the importance of marrying a Christian. She had not. Her struggles were constant reminders to us. And it hurt us, even as young children, to know that Daddy was unsaved. Being "unequally yoked" in marriage is very difficult and heartbreaking. It can also pull one away from the truth. My husband and I urge our sons, "Marry a Christian – someone who will help you go to heaven." Although Scripture does not plainly state, except for the widow, the wiser course for all is to marry "only in the Lord."

Questions

1. Why must the younger widow be refused in the enrolled widow program?

2. Did Paul condemn her for having the natural desire to remarry?

4. What would be the results if she began as an enrolled widow and then backed out?

4. A woman's life falls naturally into three periods. Describe them.

5. Why did Paul recommend the unmarried stay that way during persecution?

6. What are two possible interpretations of marry "only in the Lord"?

7. In 1 Corinthians 7:13-16, what advice does Paul give to a Christian whose unbelieving mate is content to stay with him/her? What about the unbelieving mate who leaves?

What About
The Husband Who "Obeys Not the Word"?

1 Peter 3:1-2

For 38 years, my mother experienced the frustrations of making the Christian walk alone. Like other wives of unbelieving husbands, she had to be the spiritual leader of the family. I well remember her driving our family station wagon 30 minutes to the nearest congregation in Whiteville, N.C., every Sunday and Wednesday. She probably heard little of the sermons while corralling three young daughters in the pew. But her faith was strong, and she taught us Bible stories around the kitchen table, made sure we prayed at meals, always talked positively about the church, and invited visiting preachers to our home for a meal. She taught the gospel to neighbors and filled that station wagon every trip to Whiteville. Ezekiel 16:44 tells us, "As is the mother, so is her daughter" (ASV). It's no wonder Judi and I married preachers!

My greatest source of anxiety while growing up was the fact that Daddy was not a Christian. Mama did not nag him. She told us Scripture has the answer for every problem in life. It tells us how to convert a husband and encourage him to be the spiritual leader God wants him to be. First Peter 3:1-2 gives the formula Mama practiced. Daddy was baptized in January 1992, and he remains faithful today.

God planned for every husband to be a strong spiritual leader. Steve Farrar, in his book *Point Man*, explains the divine blueprint:

The father is head of the family. Together with his wife, he raises his children in a home where Jesus Christ is the focus. The Bible is the most important book in the home. It is the responsibility of the parents, and ultimately that of the father, to make sure the children grow up in an environment that will enable them to one day become competent, responsible parents in their own right."[1]

But Satan opposes God's plan. He works through the wife to undermine the husband's leadership. Farrar aptly states that if Satan can neutralize the man (the head), he can neutralize the family. A woman helps Satan when she rejects her husband's authority. But if she wants to encourage her husband to be what God intends, she must understand the leadership traits God created within man, follow and encourage his leadership, and exemplify godly conduct.

UNDERSTAND THE LEADERSHIP TRAITS GOD CREATED WITHIN MAN

Men and women are very different. Barbara Johnson, in her book *Somewhere Between Estrogen and Death*, humorously illustrates:[2]

Ask a man where he got a cake, and he'll tell you, "At a grocery store." Ask a woman the same question and she'll ask, "What's the matter with it?"

But ask a woman how she bruised her toe, and she'll say, "I kicked a chair." Ask a man the same question, and he'll reply, "Somebody left a chair in the middle of the room!"

In Chapter 3, we discussed God's creation of the two sexes. Adam was made from the dust of the ground (Genesis 2:7), but Eve was created from his rib (vv. 21-23). Adam was designed for and given the work of tending the garden (v. 15). Not Eve. She was created as a perfectly suited companion (vv. 18-24). Headship duties were given to Adam. Since that prototype of firstborn male spiritual leadership, men have held this responsibility position in the spiritual realms of home and church. Here, women are not charged with authoritative obligations.

Because their roles and responsibilities are different, God designed men and women with gender distinctive traits – physically and emotionally. Men generally have larger muscles, broader shoulders and greater body strength for "tending the garden." In many cultures, tough manual labor is still necessary to provide for the family. Emotionally, men are "task oriented." They tend to see the big picture: bagging the bear, landing the job, conquering the enemy, or fixing the problem. Accompanying characteristics include aggressiveness and competitiveness. Other traits include resolve and independence. How many men do you know who ask for directions when they are lost?

This doesn't mean some women aren't big-boned, competitive or independent. But, in general, women possess the more feminine traits of softness, sensitivity and intuition. The God-given qualities created within men and women form two complementary dimensions so that each helps the other reach their greatest potential.

Man was naturally designed to lead because that is what God wants him to do. Tim LaHaye, in *Understanding the Male Temperament*, explains this way:

> All men possess leadership tendencies, some more than others. … [E]very man has both the capability and the desire to be a leader. … Personally, I am convinced that this is a need in every man which, if not realized, at least in his home life, will leave him unfulfilled.
>
> One goal every loving wife should have is to help her husband realize his subconscious need to be the leader of his home. No matter how passive he is, he will love her more and treat her better if he serves as their leader.[3]

To encourage leadership in men, we need to accept the masculine characteristics purposefully designed by God. Aggressiveness and competitiveness help him climb the corporate ladder and strive for the best job to provide for his family. With resolve and independence, he can ignore criticism and pressures that discourage him from fulfilling his responsibilities. These qualities are necessary for a man to be the kind of leader God wants him to be.

But Satan has convinced many women that these tendencies are bad. Thus, feminists redefine competitiveness as chauvinism, resolve as inflexibility, and independence as egotism. If a man stands firm in his leadership qualities, they call it macho arrogance. Our deceived society has discouraged these natural masculine traits and has nearly obliterated male leadership. If we want the men in our homes, churches and communities to fulfill their responsibility to lead, we must encourage the God-given characteristics in them.

FOLLOW AND ENCOURAGE HIS LEADERSHIP

A woman must also encourage her husband's attempts to lead. Men and women are equal in value before God, but they have different roles in the home (and church). Leadership responsibilities fall on the husband, even if he is not a faithful Christian. Jo Berry, in *Beloved Unbeliever*, writes, "An unequally yoked wife must respect her spouse's position as God's representative authority, trusting that He will work through her husband to accomplish His will in her life and marriage …. God is not limited because her husband doesn't believe." [4] The godly wife wants her husband to be the spiritual leader. Scripture gives the formula to convert and encourage him into obeying God's will: "Wives, likewise, be submissive to your own husbands, that even if some do not obey the word, they, without a word, may be won by the conduct of their wives, when they observe your chaste conduct accompanied by fear" (1 Peter 3:1-2 NKJV).

Peter wrote this letter to Christians scattered throughout Asia Minor. Those fleeing religious persecution were teaching the gospel wherever they went. When men were converted, wives were expected to follow their husbands' religion. But many women were converted whose husbands were not. They faced difficult circumstances. As noted earlier, Asian women were fairly independent. They were able to vote and hold public office.[5] However, according to Scot McKnight, "most scholars are agreed that when a woman struck out on her own and joined a religion different from her husband's, that could be seen as an act of insubordination."[6] In 1 Peter 3:1-2, we find Peter's instructions on how to win their husbands to the Lord.

What should the Christian woman do to lead her husband to Christ? Nagging, criticizing and demanding that he change would only aggravate the situation. Peter urges her to be submissive and behave in a godly manner that he might be persuaded. These same actions will also have a positive impact on the spiritually weak Christian husband. In this biblical recipe for encouraging the unbelieving or spiritually weak husband, Peter first commands the Christian wife to respect her husband's leadership role. She must understand that God's order of headship was established from the beginning and that although right now she is stronger spiritually, he can grow into the role God intends for him.

Because the unbelieving husband does not share his wife's Christian perspective, they may disagree on some things. But even Christian couples don't agree on everything. A good husband will have his wife's best interests at heart and will work with her in making decisions. However, if he feels he must decide against her wishes, the godly wife submits "as unto the Lord" (Ephesians 5:22 KJV). She realizes that obedience to God and harmony in the home are the more important issues. She knows that her goal is not to win the arguments but to win her husband.

Janell Smitherman, in an inspiring article titled, "Praise Your Husband Into Greatness," compares the husband learning to lead to a child learning to walk. She explains that both need reassurance and confidence from someone they love.[7] She adds, "If you are trying to encourage your husband to become a stronger head of your household, try not to advise him too much. Instead, stand by the decisions he makes, even when they're not exactly the decisions you would have made."[8] This may take an occasional leap of faith. Will you encourage him if he realizes later that he made a mistake, or will you discourage his leadership efforts by saying, "I told you so"? Do you want him to lead decisively with confidence in your support or stand paralyzed, fearing your reaction? Are you afraid he will really mess up? Remember that all things work together for good to them that love the Lord (Romans 8:28).

A nagging, critical wife discourages a husband in his attempts to lead. I know a man who led a prayer in worship and was criticized by his wife. She scolded, "That was the worst prayer I ever heard." He never led another prayer. In fact, he doesn't attend worship anymore. In fact, he isn't married to her anymore. If only she had said something positive about his effort. She could have praised his sincerity, his humble attitude, or even his courage to lead the prayer. Proverbs 14:1 tells us, "The wise woman builds her house, But the foolish tears it down with her own hands" (NASB). Smitherman writes:

> Encouragement when something is done well is many times more effective than criticizing when something is done poorly. ... Encourage the steps that your husband takes toward becoming the spiritual leader God wants him to be. ... He is not a child who needs correction. He is a man with a brilliant God-given mind, deserving of your respect. ... Pray for your husband, and believe in him.[9]

When he is admired and encouraged, he will strive to live up to what you think of him.

Because of his God-given independence and masculine pride, a man cannot be pushed or forced into change. *Fascinating Womanhood* author, Helen Andelin, identifies four reasons why a woman should not try to change her husband: [10]

(1) It creates marriage problems.

(2) It can destroy love.

(3) It can cause him to rebel.

(4) It doesn't work.

Solomon presents the negative effects of pushing your husband: "[A] nagging wife is like water that won't stop dripping" (Proverbs 17:15 ETR). "It is better to live on the roof than to live in a house with a wife that wants to argue" (21:9; 25:24 ETR). When a woman continually harps on her husband to change, he will either (1) hold tenaciously to his God-given independence by doing just the opposite, (2) he will leave, or (3) he will give up his leadership position. When constantly bombarded by discouraging words of criticism, a man with weak leadership traits will, for the sake of peace, hand that role over to his wife. Instead of a strong spiritual leader who carries the heavy burdens of headship, that woman will get a henpecked husband who withers under her reign. Then she will find herself having to carry out the leadership responsibilities. We have seen the disastrous results in our society. Tim LaHaye writes, "Unfortunately, an unnatural lifestyle of feminine-dominated homes is sweeping the land, making husbands irresponsible, wives frustrated, and children abnormal." [11]

Here is the scenario. In these homes, women reject the husband's authority. They question and contradict his decisions. Their children, observing this disrespect, show the same disdain for authority in the school and community. And the effect is that, in our society, leaders everywhere are bombarded with criticism and discouragement. Is it any wonder we have few strong, determined and decisive men willing to stand up and take the heat? How can a man lead if others will not follow? Sadly, this condition has affected the church where strong, decisive elders are so badly needed. What can we do? The answer begins in the home. Only the man who has full respect and support from his wife can stand up and lead in the home, society and the church – as God intended.

God appointed man to be head of his family (Ephesians 5:22-23), not as a dictator, but as a loving and sacrificial servant leader – as Christ is for His bride, the church. Why? Not because man is superior but because of the significance God placed upon the firstborn (1 Corinthians 11:3, 8-9; 1 Timothy 2:13-14). God will hold him accountable for leadership. Ladies, we can be encouragers of that leadership.

EXEMPLIFY GODLY CONDUCT

Finally, Peter explains that women can encourage leadership in their husbands by being godly examples. He states that husbands "without a word, may be won by the conduct of their wives" (1 Peter 3:1 NKJV), implying that these men can be influenced by some other way than words. As one scholar expressed, "The powerful purity of a godly woman's life can soften even the stoniest male heart without a word."[12] Most men will not respond positively to nagging or preaching. But God never commanded a woman to change her husband. Instead, he tells her that she must change herself (into submission and godly conduct). Then, her husband "may be won."

In the original language, "won" here means "gained" and is used to describe success in missionary activity (Matthew 18:15; 1 Corinthians 9:19-22).[13] It carries the idea of "converting" or "changing one's attitude." This is the desired result – a husband who changes his mindset from doing his own will to doing God's will. Peter says the catalyst for this change is his wife's submission and godly behavior "when they observe your chaste conduct accompanied by fear" (1 Peter 3:2 NKJV). Her husband needs to see real, joyful, attractive Christianity practiced in her everyday life. That may be the only "Bible" he reads. We have learned that "chaste" means pure in heart and mind. This is a quality that even the unbeliever can appreciate. Berry writes:

> I always have to maintain the difference between Christianity and the world, and by example, show my husband how God's way is best ... being chaste does not mean prudish or holier than thou. It means being godly, Spirit-filled.[14]

The wife's purity must be "coupled with fear [respect]." She must show reverence (respect) for God (1 Peter 1:17; 2:17-18) and for her husband (Ephesians 5:33). Peter's readers could not join their husbands in worship to the Roman gods, but they could model reverent and chaste behavior even above Roman standards.[15] Maintaining a sweet, submissive spirit will nudge unbelieving and spiritually weak husbands in the right direction.

What about the husband who slanders your religion or is defensive of his own? Submission and respect will help. Jane Kirby Smith, in her article "The Unbelieving Husband," wrote:

> He may feel left out and threatened by your dedication to live a Christian life. You must put him first whenever possible. The more secure he feels in your love, the less he will resent your attending church services and church functions."[16]

What about the children? If your husband does not fulfill his responsibilities as spiritual head of the family, then you must do all you can to ensure your own spiritual maturity and that of your children. Let me encourage you to bring them up in the Lord. Consider their eternal future. I am so thankful that my mother made the consistent effort to teach us, take us to worship, and involve us in Christian activities. Billye Christian, in "Faith of a Sunday Morning Widow," begs:

> Young mothers, I plead with you to continue to serve the Lord although your mate is not interested in the church. Yes, I know how difficult it is to get up on Sunday mornings and get yourself and the children dressed for church. Yes, I know what it feels like to go to worship services and, because of your crying babies and your misbehaving children, you get

very little out of the service. God never said that Christian life would be easy. But He did tell us that, if we served Him faithfully, we would have much joy. Mothers, when you see your precious children walk down the aisle to become Christians, then you will know real joy! [17]

If your husband is not a Christian, you can lead him to Christ. If yours is a believer but passive in his leadership role, you can encourage him. Peter advises submission and a godly example as the most effective way to impact his life.

SUMMARY

If Satan has the upper hand in his attack to neutralize your husband, defend yourself with the advice in 1 Peter 3:1-2. Understand the leadership traits God created within man, become a good follower by encouraging him into leadership, and strive to exemplify godly conduct. Respect his position as God's representative authority and treat him like a leader. When he is confident in your support, he will act like a leader. Do not push him to change. Instead, become what God wants you to be. Your husband may be won without a word when he sees how God's blueprint for the family works. Do not worry about his salvation, but pray and enlist the prayers of others. "The prayer of a righteous man is powerful and effective" (James 5:16 NIV). Place him in God's hands and never give up.

Make heaven your goal and teach your children. Isaiah's words are true: "And a little child shall lead them" (Isaiah 11:6 NKJV). In January 1992, my sister was preparing for a bone marrow transplant. Daddy, whose marrow was her closest match, was to be the donor. During their wait, she begged, "Daddy, if I die, I need to know I will see you again in heaven." Daddy was baptized that very hour. Donna was 36 years old, but she was still his child. Mama is rewarded for her early struggles raising us in the Lord – a daughter in heaven, two in ministry, and a husband finally beside her in her Christian walk.

Questions

1. What has Satan deceived feminists into believing about masculine leadership traits?

2. What three things can a wife do to encourage leadership in her husband?

3. Is submission a role for all wives or only those married to Christians? Why?

4. According to Proverbs 14:1, what does the foolish woman do?

5. List four reasons why a woman should not try to change her husband, according to our chapter.

6. What is Peter's advice to convert one's husband to the Lord without a word? Can she teach him with words?

7. What should the godly wife do for herself and her children while waiting on her husband to fulfill his spiritual leadership obligations?

What About
The Daughters of Sarah?

1 Peter 3:2-7

My first experience as a student in a ladies' Bible class was in Yuciapa, Calif., where, on Wednesday mornings, more than 60 ladies gathered to hear Alice Harriman teach Lottie Beth Hobbs' book *You Can Be Beautiful With the Beauty of Holiness.* The lessons made a tremendous impact on me. Being an impressionable 20-year-old and enamored with old movies, I could not help identifying the godly traits described in Hobbs' book with Melanie Wilkes, a character in *Gone With the Wind.* Her meek and gentle spirit was so different from the outspoken and self-assertive Scarlett O'Hara. Melanie was clothed with the inner adornment commanded by God, and this made her beautiful. In a previous lesson, we examined Paul's command against extravagant outward adornment (1 Timothy 2:9-10). Now, let us study the similar admonition from the apostle Peter.

NOT OUTWARD ADORNMENT

Peter continues his message to female converts in Asia Minor. He advised women whose husbands had not obeyed the gospel to win them by submission, godly conduct and respect (1 Peter 3:1-2). In verses 3-6, he continues to encourage Christian women in godly behavior and attitudes.

Peter's readers were under great stress, being persecuted for refusing to worship the Roman gods and, at the same time, trying to avoid appearing as the flamboyant women of the eastern cults.[1] Of course, these new converts wanted to be considered beautiful, but their culture valued elaborate hairstyles, make-up, dress and personal jewelry. They must have wondered how they could attract others to the gospel if they must look different than the exotic women around them. Hobbs writes in her forward: "Beauty has always been of universal interest to women and men alike. It is possible to develop beauty that is captivating, a calm loveliness of soul that is both sacred and compelling. God tells us how."[2]

> Your beauty should not come from outward adornment, such as braided hair and the wearing of gold jewelry and fine clothes. Instead, it should be that of your inner self, the unfading beauty of a gentle and quiet spirit, which is of great worth in God's sight (1 Peter 3:3-4 NIV).

Behavior determines true beauty. J. Ramsey Michaels writes, "A person's 'heart' is who that person is, at the deepest and most private level, and for Christian wives, according to Peter, it is the wellspring of their beauty."[3] It's what inside that counts. People will be attracted to us if we apply God's instructions. Peter's message is especially important for winning one's husband.

J.N.D. Kelly, in his commentary on First Peter, suggests that these congregations included a number of wealthy women.[4] When they became Christians, were they to dispose of all their good apparel and wear the dress of paupers? No. Peter was not prohibiting braided hair, jewels and nice clothing, any more than Paul did in his letter to Timothy. However, some ancient writers (Tertullian, Clement and Cyprian) took the text literally and taught that Peter banned feminine finery.[5] Some religious groups today also misunderstand this message. If Peter was prohibiting braids and jewelry, he was also forbidding "the putting on of apparel" (1 Peter 3:3 KJV). He was simply saying that emphasis should be on the heart, not on superficial adornment. Beauty should not come from emphasizing the outside; instead, it should be from the inside.

A MEEK AND QUIET SPIRIT

First Peter 3 separates two parts of our being: (1) The visible, physical body, which is temporal, and (2) The more precious, invisible personality, which is eternal. Paul taught that, in the Christian, this hidden "inner person" is fashioned in the likeness of Christ (Romans 7:22; 2 Corinthians 4:16; Ephesians 3:16; Colossians 3:16). Our soul cannot wear physical dress. J.W. Roberts beautifully suggests: "Being invisible, this inward personality must dress up in some manner other than stylish clothes and jewelry. The apparel it can wear is incorruptible; a meek and quiet spirit."[6] Peter is not talking about the Holy Spirit here but a woman's disposition. Such a sweet spirit speaks for itself. A woman with this beautiful characteristic does not have to show off with perishable gold and finery. Her inner beauty attracts others to the gospel with meekness and quietness.

Peter still has in mind the woman who desires to convert her pagan husband. This man should be able to see holiness in her demeanor. McKnight writes: "The 'quiet spirit' Peter enjoins here is that Christian wives avoid a cantankerous grumbling that would prevent a non-Christian husband from seeing God's grace and goodness in her behavior."[7] He will certainly not be drawn to Christianity if she is angry or sarcastic when he belittles her religion. Paul gave a similar message to Timothy: "I urge ... that we may live peaceful and quiet lives in all godliness and holiness ... [because] God ... wants all men to be saved and to come to a knowledge of the truth" (1 Timothy 2:2-4 NIV).

Peter notes that, in contrast to the world's admiration of expensive dress, God regards the Christian disposition of a meek and quiet spirit as very precious. So does her husband. "Who can find a virtuous wife? For her worth is far above rubies" (Proverbs 31:10 NKJV). The Greek term Peter uses for "very precious" (1 Peter 3:4 NKJV) means "of great worth, valuable." It is the same word used to describe the costly oil poured on Jesus' head in Mark 14:3. That perfume was so expensive that it could have been sold for more than a year's wages (vv. 4-5). The godly woman who clothes her soul with God-pleasing, very precious adornment will wear it throughout eternity in her heavenly home. She will also keep her husband's affection and perhaps win him to Christ.

HOLY WOMEN OF THE PAST

Next, Peter points to beautiful Old Testament women who chose a meek and quiet spirit over outward extravagance.

> For in this manner, in former times, the holy women who trusted in God also adorned themselves, being submissive to their own husbands, as Sarah obeyed Abraham, calling him lord, whose daughters you are if you do good and are not afraid with any terror (1 Peter 3:5-6 NKJV).

Just like Peter's female readers, those women of the past were holy or set apart. One commentator suggests the apostle may have had in mind the four matriarchs: Sarah (wife of Abraham), Rebekah (wife of Isaac), and Rachel and Leah (the two wives of Jacob).[8] Surely the new converts of Asia Minor had read about these women in the Old Testament. Their stories illustrate their faith in God.

Peter wanted to encourage women who may suffer harassment for their faith. He urges them to put their hope in God and keep their eyes on heaven. One scholar writes:

> Earlier in his letter Peter affirmed that believers, whose hope is in God, look forward to a future inheritance and salvation in spite of suffering in all kinds of trials (1:3-6, 13, 21). This is the same hope entertained by holy women of old who trusted in God, looking forward to His future redemption, a redemption Peter knew had been realized in Christ but would be fulfilled when He returns.[9]

Peter urges Christian women to imitate them.

In 1 Peter 3:5, he describes them as "being submissive to their own husbands" (NKJV). The worthy Old Testament examples acknowledged their husbands' leadership. Peter singles out Sarah saying she "obeyed Abraham, calling him lord" (v. 6). The word "lord" here means "one in authority." This is an important distinction because in ancient literature "lord" was not commonly used for husbands.[10] Sarah's attitude of respect was a habitual disposition, as shown by the continuous participle "calling" him lord, which is used in most versions, instead of "called" him lord. Throughout the Genesis account of Abraham and

Sarah, we see her deference toward him. Yet, we find only one account of her calling Abraham "lord." In Genesis 18, Sarah overheard the promise that she would bear a son. She laughed to herself as she thought, "After I have grown old, shall I have pleasure, my lord being old also?" (v. 12 NKJV). Coffman points out the significance of Sarah calling her husband 'lord' in her thoughts, "[T]his is what she called him in her own heart, not merely when others might hear her." [11] Sarah submitted to her husband, and he, in turn, showed respect toward her. When she asked him to lie with her maidservant, Hagar, in order to bear him a child, he "agreed to what Sarai said" (Genesis 16:2 NIV). When she said, "Get rid of that slave woman and her son," God told Abraham to listen to "whatever Sarah tells you" (21:10, 12 NIV). The honor and respect shown by this couple were mutual.

DAUGHTERS OF SARAH

Peter concludes his thoughts on Sarah by stating, "You are her daughters if you do what is right and do not give way to fear" (1 Peter 3:6 NIV). Unlike the Jews who were born from the seed of Abraham, these new Gentile converts became children of Abraham (spiritual Israel) when they were baptized (Romans 4:11; Galatians 3:7). In the same way, Christian women have become spiritual daughters of Sarah. But notice the condition – "if you do what is right ["do good," NKJV] and do not give way to fear ["not afraid with any terror" NKJV]." [12] If we would truly be daughters of Sarah, we must do good by imitating her submission to authority and her courage in the face of trying circumstances. How far does obedience go when one is married to an unbeliever? Michaels explains:

> A Christian wife's deference to her pagan husband cannot extend to adopting his religion, for this would be a failure to "do good." If she "does good" by maintaining her allegiance to God even while showing deference to her husband, there is always a possibility, however remote, that her husband may not understand or tolerate her alien religion and that consequently her freedom or safety may be jeopardized. Hence the ominous word of "comfort" with which

Peter's advice to wives concludes: "and let nothing frighten you" (lit., "not fearing any terror").[13]

The phrase "not fearing any terror" has special meaning for those being harassed for their faith. The Greek word for terror is not the same as the word for calm and thoughtful fear.[14] It literally meant "anything sudden that might startle in a frightening way." We see this clearly in Proverbs 3:25: "Do not be afraid of sudden terror, Nor of trouble from the wicked when it comes" (NKJV; see also Luke 21:9 KJV; Luke 24:37 NIV). The terror Peter refers to here is probably the intimidation this Christian wife might receive from her unsaved husband. Just a few verses after this, Peter writes, "And who is there to harm you if you prove zealous for what is good? But even if you should suffer for the sake of righteousness, you are blessed. And do not fear their intimidation, and do not be troubled" (1 Peter 3:13-14 NASB).

These were comforting words to the readers. When these women left the common religions of their culture and accepted Christianity, they risked harsh retaliation from their unbelieving family and friends. *The Pulpit Commentary* describes their situation:

> From time to time one member of a family circle would have to put the constraining love of Christ above the love due to father or mother, husband, wife, or child. The case of a Christian wife with an unbelieving husband would be one of special difficulty. She would probably have to hear her religion derided, her Savior insulted; she would have to endure constant reproaches and sarcasms, often hardships, and even brutal cruelty.[15]

This message is very relevant today. Many Christian women struggle with similar intimidation. They need our encouragement. Fred Craddock offers:

> Implied in this instruction, however, is that one is not to relinquish one's faith because a domineering and threatening husband demands it. If the line is drawn there, we have no word from the writer to wives who might find themselves divorced by such husbands. Paul's advice was: Stay with

your spouse but if he (or she) divorces you, then you are no longer under obligation; you are free (1 Corinthians 7:15).[16] Although Sarah's husband was not a pagan, she did submit to his authority in many unjust and dangerous situations. She pulled up roots and followed him to a new home. She pretended to be his sister as he asked when they entered the courts of Pharaoh and Abimelech (Genesis 12; 20). She may have known about God's request for the sacrifice of Isaac as she watched Abraham take their son to Mount Moriah. It appears that Peter is urging Christian wives to imitate Sarah's submissive obedience even in the middle of unjust and frightening situations. It would be a wonderful thing to be enough like Sarah to be called "her daughter." What faith she had in God. What respect she showed her husband. How blessed she was. She is one of only two women God saw fit to name in the list of Old Testament faithfuls in Hebrews 11. She is worthy of imitation.

PETER'S MESSAGE TO CHRISTIAN HUSBANDS

In 1 Peter 3:7 of our text, Peter explains how Christian men are to treat their wives:

> Husbands, in the same way be considerate as you live with your wives, and treat them with respect as the weaker partner and as heirs with you of the gracious gift of life, so that nothing will hinder your prayers (NIV).

"In the same way" – husbands also have a responsibility in promoting a spiritually healthy marriage. Paul does not discuss how to convert wives because in that culture a woman normally accepted the religion of her husband. The problem Peter deals with is the selfish, domineering attitude held by pagan men.

> In the first century, there was frequent divorce among Jews and heathens, a dislike of marriage among the Romans, and the Greeks regarded the wife as mistress of the house and mother of the children, but not as a helper and companion. Womanhood was depreciated. Marriage was very different from what God intended it to be.[17]

These husbands needed to realize that Christianity entitled women to the same relationship with God as men (Galatians 3:28). Peter calls the Christian husband and wife co-heirs. It was not easy for these first generation Christian men to view their wives in such light. They understood headship, but Peter explains to them its limitations. They needed to learn to treat their wives in a new manner. Mutual respect is the message here. Paul had preached sacrificial love on the part of husbands in the Ephesian letter (Ephesians 5:24-25). Peter adds understanding and honor. The husband must learn to "dwell" (NKJV) with her (specifically in the sexual relationship, and more broadly in day-to-day living together), having a biblical view of marriage instead of his former pagan perspective.[18] A truly spiritual husband will consider her feelings, behave as a gentleman, and understand that his wife was given a more delicate frame (a different form for a different function). She is called "the weaker vessel." The Greek term for "vessel" literally meant "a piece of pottery or a jar (a container)," but was used metaphorically in scripture to mean "the container of the soul" or "the human body."[19] Peter says the husband must not misuse his leadership role by taking physical advantage of his wife. Barnes suggests:

> She may have mental endowments equal to his own; she may have moral qualities in every way superior to his; but the God of nature has made her with a more delicate frame, a more fragile structure, and with a body subject to many infirmities to which the more hardy frame of a man is stranger.[20]

The Christian husband is to treat his wife with honor and respect because she is his sister in Christ – joint heirs in the blessed hope of eternal life. When they treat each other the way God commands, He will hear their prayers. But He will not listen if arguing and fighting mar their relationship. Jesus said, "Therefore if you bring your gift to the altar, and there remember that your brother has something against you, leave your gift there before the altar, and go your way. First be reconciled to your brother, and then come and offer your gift" (Matthew 5:23-24 NKJV).

SUMMARY

I still watch *Gone With the Wind* and admire the beautiful Melanie Wilkes. But Sarah is the model of Peter's choice. She and other holy women of the past made themselves beautiful by modeling submission, godly conduct and respect. They dressed their inner being with a meek and quiet spirit and did not fear any frightening circumstances that came their way. They hoped in God. As Christians, we become Sarah's spiritual daughters if we truly imitate her example. Submission and respect are the keys to a Christian marriage. Both husband and wife, as joint heirs, share in this responsibility. Peter wrote his letter to encourage new converts coming out of paganism. His words support many principles we have learned from the pen of Paul.

Nearly 30 years have passed since our wonderful ladies class studied Lottie Beth's book. As I stand before my bookshelf of favorite ladies class books, I fondly turn the pages of my worn copy. Scrawled in the margins are special notes written long ago by my young and eager hands. The lessons in that book are still relevant, for they come from God's timeless, inspired Scriptures. Sister Hobbs captured the messages of Peter and Paul: *You Can Be Beautiful With the Beauty of Holiness.*

Questions

1. What determines true beauty?

2. Name some women whom you consider beautiful with the beauty of holiness.

3. How might one determine whether she is adorned with too much feminine finery?

4. What two parts of our being does Peter discuss? How should each be clothed?

5. Discuss the meaning of the term "very precious" used to describe a meek and quiet spirit.

6. What terms does Peter use to describe the holy women of the past?

7. How should a woman handle harassment from her unbelieving husband and friends?

8. What must we do to be called true daughters of Sarah?

9. Discuss some frightening situations the wife of an unbelieving husband may face.

10. Compare the views of headship a pagan husband might have with what the Christian husband should have.

What About
The Deaconess?

Romans 16:1; 1 Timothy 3:8-12

The following announcement appeared in an Alabama congregation's bulletin:

> We will appoint deacons for this church on Pentecost Sunday
> .... Deacons will be male and female. On Sunday nights and
> Wednesday nights and Sunday morning Bible classes, shared
> leadership in the services will continue .... Men and women
> can occupy any roles in the leadership of our fellowship.[1]

Does the Bible authorize the official appointment of deaconesses? In this lesson we will explore the word "deaconess," two scriptures that some claim refer to the deaconess, and the background of deaconesses in church history.

THE WORD "DEACONESS"

What do you think when you hear the term "deaconess"? There may be varying opinions even among those in your Bible class. Webster defines it as "a woman elected or appointed to serve as an assistant in a church." The MSN Encarta on-line dictionary describes her as a "woman with duties of a deacon: a woman who ranks below a priest or who is appointed to assist a minister."[2] In this study, we will cover a variety of meanings by examining whether a woman may be a servant in the church, whether she can be appointed as a servant, and whether such an appointment may include an official, technical position – a female deacon.

We do not find the word "deaconess" in Scripture, except in a few versions of Romans 16:1 (such as the RSV) where Paul describes a Christian woman named Phoebe. Most translations have rendered the original word "servant" in this verse. Romans 16:1 reads:

> I commend to you Phoebe our sister, who is a servant [deaconess, RSV] of the church in Cenchrea, that you may receive her in the Lord in a manner worthy of the saints, and assist her in whatever business she has need of you; for indeed she has been a helper of many and of myself also (NKJV).

Does the term "deaconess" correctly describe Phoebe, or does the RSV overstep scriptural boundaries? The original term used by Paul (*diakonos*) simply meant "servant," and could apply to a male or female. Appearing about 30 times in the Greek New Testament, this word is translated into English in three different senses.

(1) *Servant.* Scholars translated the word as servant when describing one who waits at a meal (John 2:5, 9), serves a master (Matthew 22:13), or serves another (Mark 9:35). For example: "But he who is greatest among you shall be your servant (Matthew 23:11 NKJV).

(2) *Minister.* The same word is rendered minister for a person serving God or Christ as in 1 Corinthians 3:5: "Who then is Paul, and who is Apollos, but ministers through whom you believed, as the Lord gave to each one?" (NKJV; also Romans 13:4; Ephesians 3:7; 6:21; Colossians 1:23).

(3) *Deacon.* Translators transliterated the word "deacon" from the original term to represent an officially appointed servant of the church. "Let deacons be the husbands of one wife, ruling their children and their own houses well" (1 Timothy 3:12 NKJV). Philippians 1:1 implies a distinction of this group from the elders and other saints.

All three senses come from the same Greek word. Which sense did Paul have in mind when he described Phoebe? The RSV, by using a feminine form of the third, technical sense (deaconess), may imply that

Phoebe served in an officially appointed position. Can we determine from Romans 16:1 that this is what Paul meant?

PHOEBE'S STATUS

Phoebe lived in Rome. We noted in our study of the Corinthians that many Roman women enjoyed wealth and status. Some, called patrons, had power and influence. From Paul's words, we can infer that Phoebe was such a patron who served others in the church. He writes, "[F]or indeed she has been a helper of many and of myself also" (Romans 16:2 NKJV). The word translated "helper" meant "benefactor, succorer (KJV), good friend." This term, "*prostatis*" (patron, helper), according to Everett Ferguson, is even more noteworthy in describing Phoebe than *diakonos* (servant, minister, deacon).

Of more significance for Phoebe's status and influence is the description of her as *prostatis*, the feminine of a word for a leader, ruler, president, guardian, and in Greek and Roman society a patron. This indicates that Phoebe was a person of some wealth and social standing, and it is likely that she owned a home that provided a meeting place for the church and hospitality to Paul and other Christians. This would have given her considerable prominence if not an officially recognized position in the church.[3]

Because of her social position, Phoebe was able to render service to Paul and others in the church. And because Paul used the term "*diakonos*" (servant, minister, deacon) to describe her, we are certain she did offer service in some way. But this is all we know. Romans 16:1 does not offer enough evidence to confirm she held any special role or that she was even appointed to serve the church in any capacity. Guy N. Woods suggests that "the designation is functional and denotes the work she did, and not an office she held."[4] Her work of service was greatly appreciated by Paul and others in the church at Cenchrea.

"THE WOMEN" IN 1 TIMOTHY 3:11

Another scripture some claim as describing deaconesses in the church is 1 Timothy 3:11. We have already discussed 1 Timothy as Paul's in-

struction manual for church leaders. In verses 1-13, he gives qualifications for elders and deacons. Focusing on deacons in verses 8-13,
he describes male candidates who must be the husband of one wife
(v. 12). But in verse 11, he interjects qualifications for certain females.

> Deacons likewise must be serious, not double-tongued, not
> addicted to much wine, not greedy for gain; they must hold
> the mystery of the faith with a clear conscience. And let
> them also be tested first; then if they prove themselves blame-
> less let them serve as deacons (1 Timothy 3:8 RSV).

> The women [wives, KJV, NKJV] likewise must be serious, no
> slanderers, but temperate, faithful in all things (v. 11).

> Let deacons be married only once, and let them manage their
> children and their households well; for those who serve well
> as deacons gain a good standing for themselves and also great
> confidence in the faith which is in Christ Jesus (v. 12).

Paul uses the Greek word "*gune*," the same word for woman and wife.
Is Paul referring to the wives of the deacons here or is he talking about
certain women who served in the church? We know there were females
who served in the church such as the enrolled widows (see Chapter 8).

Some scholars believe Paul was referring to wives of deacons.[5] The
description does fall in the middle of a discussion about male deacons.
Warren Wiersbe notes: "The deacon's wife is a part of his ministry, for
godliness must begin at home. ... Their wives must be Christians,
women who are serious about the ministry, not given to slanderous talk
... and faithful in all that they do."[6] Marvin Vincent, in *Word Studies
in the New Testament*, agrees. "A Deacon whose wife is wanting in the
qualities required in him is not to be chosen. She would sustain an
active relation to his office, and by her ministries would increase his
efficiency, and by frivolity, slander, or intemperance, would bring him
and his office into disrepute.[7]

We must consider the fact that Paul used *gune* (woman, wife) and
not *diakonos* (servant, minister, deacon). Burton Coffman writes, "In
this connection, it is proper to note that if Paul had meant these women
to be installed as 'deaconesses' he certainly knew the word and would

have referred to them in this passage by their proper title."[8] Paul may have meant wives.

However, some scholars believe Paul may have been referring to a special group of women servants.[9] They claim Paul interrupts his discussion of the male deacons to give qualifications for the female servants. Everett Ferguson suggests that the following structure may indicate Paul's parallel instructions:[10]

Now a bishop must be …	(3:2)
Deacons likewise must be …	(3:8)
The women likewise must be …	(3:11)

He explains that the word "women" may seem out of place here in its general meaning, and adds, "No biblical principle appears to prohibit the recognition of women in serving capacities in a church … women servants in a non-technical sense is perhaps not out of the question."[11] Barclay offers:

> As far as the Greek goes, this could refer to the wives of the deacons, or to women who are engaged in a similar service. It seems far more likely that it refers to women who are also engaged upon this work of charity. There must have been acts of kindness and of help which only a woman could properly do for another woman.[12]

Robert R. Taylor adds that such female servants may have been asked by the elders to take care of special needs:

> It is my seasoned conviction that Paul here is speaking of a group of female servants who were employed by the church to engage in such work as alone they can do … . In ministering to these of their own sex, and doing the type of teaching that Paul enjoins in Titus 2:3-5, they would be going from house to house and would need certain well ordered qualifications … . Women were appointed by elders for just such works in the first century and still are by elders today.[13]

Again, we know female servants were in the church, such as the enrolled widows. Perhaps Paul was referring to them here. But we cannot be sure. He may have meant wives. If he meant wives, did he mean deacons' wives only, as the placement of his instructions suggests? Or was he including elders' wives? If we could be certain Paul meant wives, we would end our study here, for no other verses are used to support deaconesses. But the ambiguity of the language and structure of 1 Timothy 3:11 prevents any certain interpretation. To be diligent, we must consider the possibility that Paul meant female servants. Were they appointed? Did he think of them as counterparts to male deacons? Or was he merely presenting standards for their people-oriented service?

BIBLICAL EVIDENCE

Acts 6 records an instance of seven men being chosen for special service. They were specially selected to care for the neglected Grecian widows. The term "deacon" is not found in this passage. However, in *An Expository Dictionary of New Testament Words*, W.E. Vine explains: "The so-called 'seven deacons' in Acts 6 are not there mentioned by that name, though the kind of service in which they were engaged was of the character of that committed to such."[14] This recorded appointment serves as a biblical example still followed by the Lord's church today. These men we call deacons were appointed to meet a special need. There is room for debate about whether deacons hold "an office," but these men were officially recognized. Is there a similar example of female appointments?

The only biblical example of women specifically being named for special service are the enrolled widows in 1 Timothy 5:1-10. We noted in our lesson on widows that, according to an early third-century document, "when a widow is appointed, she is not ordained but she shall be chosen by name."[15] The fact that she was not ordained confirms that these female servants did not hold a technical, official position. So, if the enrolled widows (the only biblical example of appointed female servants) did not occupy an official position, we cannot assume that female servants in 1 Timothy 3:11 did. The evidence is simply not there.

DEACONESSES IN EARLY CHURCH HISTORY

We have cited that the only documentation of appointed female servants in scripture is the enrolled widow. Paul may have been referring to this group in 1 Timothy 3:11. And we know other women, such as Phoebe, served the church, although there is no evidence of official appointment. Before the third century, the only historical evidence for female servants in the early church is found in a letter, written around A.D. 112, by Pliny the Younger, governor of Bithynia. He wrote to Emperor Trajan during Roman persecution of Christians. The letter discusses two Christian women being tortured for information about Christian activities. Pliny refers to these women as "female maidservants" called *ministrae* (Latin), often translated deaconesses. But no other information is given about them, their work or any official appointment or position.

We do not find any real references to deaconess until some time after A.D. 200. Such references show that between the second and fourth centuries, an "order of deaconesses" evolved. *The Interpreters' Dictionary of the Bible* tells us that this "order" does not appear to have existed in the church of Rome.[16] How did it begin? The Catholic online encyclopedia reveals: "Most Catholic scholars incline to the view that it is not always possible to draw a clear distinction in the early Church between deaconesses and widows."[17] Third century records that describe the work of a female *diakonos* (servant, minister, deacon) list the same duties as that of enrolled widows. Ferguson explains one such text, the Syriac *Didascalia Apostolorium*, chapter 16, written about A.D. 200-240:

> The Syriac *Didascalia* 16 uses "deaconess" for a woman appointed for ministry to women, care for the sick, and assistance at the baptism of women, including instruction of these newly baptized women in pure and holy behavior. These women deacons are distinct from the widows ... and are the counterpart of male deacons, who serve under the bishop in other matters. The name "deaconesses" was a newly coined title.[18]

These third-century documents did not use a feminine form of the Greek word "*diakonos*." Sandifer states, "It is only in the fourth century, beginning with Apostolic Constitutions, that the word 'deaconess' is coined for the female ministry."[19]

The Catholic on-line encyclopedia makes an interesting point.

> It is probable … that in the earlier period it was only a widow who could become a deaconess, but undoubtedly the strict limits of age, sixty years, which were at first prescribed for widows, were relaxed, at least at certain periods and in certain localities, in the case of those to be appointed to be deaconesses.[20]

The scriptural qualifications of enrolled widows apparently became diluted in this evolving "order" of deaconesses. Decrees from the Councils of Chalcedon (A.D. 451) and Trullo (A.D. 692) show a change in the age of eligibility from 60 years old to 40.[21] We have an account of Tertullian rebuking the ordination of a 20-year old virgin to "the order of widows" around A.D. 208-217.

We should note that even in early records of the "order" of deaconess, the role remained service-oriented. Documents show that these female servants were forbidden to teach men, baptize or have anything to do with the sacramental functions reserved for men.[22] The Catholic on-line encyclopedia indicates that the status of women-helpers (deaconesses) was "obscure and confused."[23] By the fourth century, the role had apparently developed into an official position. But, according to the *International Standard Bible Encyclopedia*, abuses of the position gradually became prevalent.[24] The abuses reached a point where the "order" had to be repressed by conciliar decrees. The 19th canon of the Council of Nicaea (A.D. 325) decreed that deaconesses would be accounted as lay persons and that they receive no ordination.[25] Another, the 11th canon of Laodicea (A.D. 343-381), declared a prohibition of the appointment of deaconesses.[26] Even the denominational world understood biblical limitations on women's roles and that no divine authority existed for the appointment of deaconesses.

The questions of our lesson are answered: (1) Yes, a woman may be a servant in the church; (2) The only example of appointed female servants in the early church is the enrolled widow; and (3) There is no biblical example of any woman being appointed to an official, technical position (a female deacon). Yet, there are many ways a woman can serve without being appointed or given a title.

THE DEACONESS TODAY

So, what about the deaconess? Some churches, even in our brotherhood, are officially appointing female servants today. Even if they do not use the term "deaconess," they should first consider some serious issues of biblical authority, limitations and influence.

• *Biblical Authority.* Other than enrolled widows, no biblical evidence exists for appointing female servants (*diakonos* – servant, minister, deacon). Coffman explains, "When women deacons are appointed, they are appointed without divine authority and with no adequate list of qualifications to serve as guidelines for their appointment."[27] Every generation produces students of the Bible who question and restudy doctrinal issues (instrumental music, baptism, etc.). Have godly Christians in past generations purposefully suppressed the appointment of women servants? No. Sincere students of the Bible have understood this issue since the first century. Our generation must not remove the old landmarks and disregard the wisdom of such mentors as Gus Nichols, who wrote:

> I know of no Bible authority to have women fill some office in the church, in the sense that we think of the elders and deacons. There is nothing said of the selection and appointment of women to an official position in the church. No qualifications are recorded for such an appointment. ...
>
> Even the performance of some special work in the church for which some good sister may be fitted would not demand that she be appointed to some office in the church not mentioned in the Scriptures. Good Christian women may be employed by the church, or do good work in the church without charge, if they can do so, but where is the authority for having them selected and appointed in some office in the church? [28]

If we follow the only biblical authorization given for choosing female servants, we would choose widows over the age of 60, who had only had one husband, and who are well reported of good works. She must be serious, not a slanderer, but temperate, faithful in all things. And we must be prepared to support her financially in her ministry of service to women, children and the sick and needy. If any point to

1 Timothy 3:11 and favor the recognition of other female servants, they should study the problems in the early century "order" of deaconesses and continually review biblical limitations on women's role.

• *Limitations.* Carrol R. Sutton, in *Guardian of Truth*, presents food for thought:

> Women certainly have the right to engage in any authorized work so long as they do not violate some scriptural principle in so doing. ... All of us should make sure that we do not encourage women to go beyond the limits God has placed upon them. Let us also be sure that we are not guilty of binding restrictions upon women that God has not bound.[29]

Female servants, just as other women in the church, must never go beyond scriptural limitations. They are not to teach nor have authority over a man (1 Timothy 2:12). They are to keep silent in the assembly (1 Corinthians 14:34-36). They must recognize their assigned role in the authority/submission order established from the beginning (Genesis 2:18; 3:16; 1 Corinthians 11:3, 8-9; 14:34-35; 1 Timothy 2:13-14). These scriptural principles must be followed no matter what role, ministry or activities they participate in in the New Testament church. Olbricht observes:

> Even if we could establish that the office of deaconess existed, this would not prove that women served as overseers in the early church. Such evidence would not confirm that women did all the other things some people speculate that they did, nor would it uphold all the practices regarding women's roles that some are permitting today.[30]

Even female servants in the third and fourth century "order of deaconesses" who exerted roles of ministry beyond biblical limitations had their ordination repealed and their appointments cancelled.

• *Influence.* We have no proof that women were ever officially appointed as deaconesses in the New Testament church. The term describing Phoebe was not translated "deaconess" until the 20th century, and even then only by a few. Opinions are divided over the women referred to in 1 Timothy 3:11. Taylor comments: "To see in this verse any warrant or support for a group of official deaconesses, as a number of religious bodies practice, is, in our judgment, to read far too much into the passage. The authorization for such is just not there."[31] The RSV's description of Phoebe as a deaconess may be linguistically acceptable. The NIV actually includes the word deaconess in its margin of this passage. If everyone defined the term "deaconess" simply as "a female servant," we might agree. Woods suggested:

> Many congregations have faithful sisters especially qualified to whom the elders turn when needs arise which neither they nor the deacons are suited to do. And, it is not out of order to refer to women in this category as deaconesses. This is a scriptural term and denotes a scriptural work. In a day when many congregations have 'ministers of education,' 'ministers of youth,' 'ministers of music,' none of which terms is found in the New Testament either in Greek or in English, we ought not to oppose the proper use of a term dictated by the Holy Spirit![32]

Let me hasten to add that Woods wrote concerning 1 Timothy 3:11: "There is no support here, or elsewhere in the sacred writings, for the practice engaged in by some religious bodies of appointed women as official deaconesses."[33]

Paul used the word "*diakonos*" (servant, minister, deacon) to describe Phoebe, and she was a female. If there was a feminine form of the word "*diakonos*," it could be translated female servant, female minister or female deacon, depending on Paul's meaning. If we assumed the third sense – female deacon – we must remember that a male deacon represents a technical, officially appointed position. And there is no biblical authority for such a female position.

What does the word "deaconess" bring to mind in the 21st century religious world? Let us review the MSN Encarta on-line dictionary definition: a "woman with duties of a deacon; a woman who ranks below a priest or who is appointed to assist a minister." It does not define deaconess as "a female servant." It implies a position for which there is no biblical authority. If we call female servants "deaconesses" today, those outside the Lord's church may misinterpret the title. It would be very easy for some to assume these female servants hold a technical, official position. And that concept is unbiblical.

Summary

Should a woman feel robbed of her talents if she is not officially appointed to the role of female servant or deaconess? Wiersbe beautifully states: "It is not necessary to hold an office to have a ministry or exercise a gift."[34] Should she feel discriminated against if she is not given such titles? Not if she is a servant in the true sense of the word. Our heavenly reward will not be based on a role title or whether others even recognize our work but on our faithful service whenever and wherever opportunities arise. Steven Sandifer well describes the woman who serves when he said of Phoebe, "She is a model of servant leadership … . That is the work of a deacon with or without the title."[35]

Questions

1. What two scriptures are used by some to refer to deaconesses in the early church?

2. In what three senses is the Greek term "*diakonos*" translated in Scripture?

3. What "more significant term" describes Phoebe, and what does it indicate about her?

4. The word "women" in Paul's discussion of deacons (1 Timothy 3:11) may indicate either of two female groups. Who are they?

5. Does Romans 16:1 offer enough evidence to prove that Phoebe occupied an officially appointed position?

6. In what century do we first find historical evidence of an "order" of deaconesses? How might such an official position have developed?

7. May female servants go beyond the limitations God has placed on other Christian women in church life?

8. Why is it unwise for female servants to wear the name deaconess today?

What About
The Women?

A Summary

What about the women? God has called us to be servants in realms of ministry as older women, younger women, wives, mothers, worshipers, widows, servants – Christians. We were created as a help – a responder to the needs of others. This is where we find our greatest blessings. When Jesus' apostles wondered who would wash their feet, Jesus picked up a towel and humbly served. His message was, "[W]hoever would be great among you must be your servant" (Mark 10:44 ESV). The New Testament passages we have studied present God's instructions on how women can best serve acceptably before God.

We share a submissive role in God's hierarchical order – not the more difficult one – but one that offers us freedom from many burdens and responsibilities God requires of men. Male spiritual leadership in the home and in the church is God's protective umbrella that ensures our spiritual and physical needs are met. Satan deceived Eve in this matter, and he works very hard to draw our attention away from God's plan. The scriptures concerning women bring it back into focus.

OLDER WOMEN, TEACH THE YOUNGER WOMEN (Titus 2:3-5)

We began with the Bible-based training program for young wives and mothers in Titus 2:3-5. The older, mature and experienced women are to train the younger in practical, biblical answers to life's challenges.

Paul urged the older women to be reverent in behavior, not slanderers, not addicted to wine, and teachers of good things. They are to encourage the younger women to understand the seriousness of their role as wives and mothers. Paul presents a seven-course curriculum necessary for maintaining spiritually healthy homes. The younger women must learn to love their husbands and children with tender, affectionate *phileo* love. This helps ensure healthy marriages and well-adjusted children. They also should learn to be moderate (self-controlled) in all they do and to be pure in heart and mind. They desire to learn the joys of homemaking with heartfelt priority. It is an important work of meaningful activities that creates a loving and peaceful haven where our families can recuperate from the world. Younger women should learn to be kind. And they need to understand that God's blueprint for the home calls for male spiritual leadership. This protects her from heavy burdens that fall on the head of the house. Older women, teach the younger women that these attitudes and behaviors are the secrets for developing spiritually healthy lives and homes.

WIVES, SUBMIT TO YOUR OWN HUSBANDS (Ephesians 5:22-23)

At creation, woman was designed differently from her husband in form and function. Adam and Eve were given characteristics and tendencies that fit them for their differing roles. As firstborn, man was given the role of male spiritual leadership. Woman was created as a perfectly suited companion. When Eve listened to Satan and led her husband into sin, she wrongfully took the spiritual leadership role; yet Adam passively complied with her wishes. Their sins negatively affected three realities of life: man's work, woman's childbearing and the marital relationship.

God expects man, as created firstborn, to fulfill spiritual leadership responsibilities in the home (Ephesians 5:22-23). He formally declared to Eve the wife's submissive role (Genesis 3:16; Ephesians 5:22-23; Colossians 3:18; Titus 2:4-5). Submission is defined as a voluntary subordination to a recognized authority. Even the secular world understands this. Smoothly running businesses, schools, government and militia are all organized with authoritative and submissive roles. All are equal as human beings. They simply have different roles in their organizations.

Satan has deceived many today into believing that submission to one's husband is degrading, that it implies inferiority or enslavement. Not so. It is liberating. It places the physical and emotional pressures of the household where they belong – on the head. God never commanded anything that wasn't good. Submission has inherent blessings. The woman who follows God's plan for the home has a husband who is free to lead and children who learn to respect authority. The woman who chooses not to obey God has Eve's lost paradise as her example.

SHE OUGHT TO HAVE AUTHORITY ON HER HEAD (1 Corinthians 11:2-16)

The concept of male spiritual leadership extends from the home to a larger family – the church. In this spiritual realm, the authority/submission order must be recognized. When the Christian women of Corinth questioned the necessity of the veil (their cultural symbol of submission), Paul defended its use. He reaffirmed the divine hierarchical order: God, Christ, man, woman. Christianity did not affect that order as some believe Galatians 3:28 teaches. Its message is that Christianity opened the door for everyone to have a personal relationship with God through Christ, even those previously restricted – women, slaves, Gentiles.

If the Corinthian women removed their veils, it would appear as insubordination. Reputable women covered their heads in public. Worshiping without the veil was shameful. Paul said that if a woman would embarrass herself in this way, she might as well cut her hair, which was also considered shameful, and be totally disgraced. By not covering her head in worship, she dishonored her authoritative head – man. He is the image and glory of God because of creation order and purpose. Therefore, Paul said the women ought to wear the cultural symbol that showed recognition of that authority.

The veil also showed a distinction between male and female. God requires that distinction to be seen. His natural gift of long hair for women has been generally recognized as a female distinction. "Long" is a relative term, but if a woman has long hair that distinguishes her from a man "it is a glory to her; for her hair is given her instead of a covering" (1 Corinthians 11:15 NKJV).

Male/female distinctiveness and authority/submission order must be demonstrated today. We have cultural symbols that show a wife's submission. But, in worship, we do not have one. Simmons suggests, "If a symbol is to be maintained, a suitable alternative to the wearing of head coverings could be the presence of a male leader in the services in which women participate."[1] This is precisely what Paul prescribes, as a commandment of the Lord, later in this letter to the Corinthians (14:37).

LET THE WOMEN BE SILENT IN THE ASSEMBLY (1 Corinthians 14:33-35)

We must demonstrate God's authority/submission order in worship. Ferguson correctly observed, "The [worship] assembly exemplifies the church as the people of God. Hence, there should be a representation of God's appointed order."[2] Because we do not have a cultural symbol of submission, how can we show it? Ferguson says, "Every time a man instead of a woman speaks to the assembled church, the divine order is thus demonstrated. The different functions assigned men and women in the assembly are a sign of the created order."[3]

"Let the women keep silence in the churches" (1 Corinthians 14:34 ASV). Silence in the assembly declares loudly and clearly to all that we, as women, acknowledge God's prescribed male spiritual leadership. Paul told the Corinthians that silence is commanded because of the authority/submission order established at creation and grounded in the law (vv. 34-35; 1 Timothy 2:11-14). As a whole, godly women outnumber men in church membership. Many are more spiritual, more intelligent and even more talented. But the principle of firstborn male spiritual leadership was never based on spirituality or ability. It has more to do with responsibility than privilege. God is not trying to suppress women by requiring silence in the assembly. They may use their talents in so many other ways. But He has given one restriction. Women must voluntarily be silent and allow the men to fulfill their God-given responsibilities to lead in spiritual matters. All activities in the assembly involving women must be viewed in light of the authority/submission order. Those who ignore this command will not be recognized.

SHE MUST NOT TEACH, NOR HAVE AUTHORITY OVER A MAN (1 Timothy 2:12)

Women's silence is commanded specifically for the assembly (when the whole church comes together, 1 Corinthians 11:18, 14:34). But in

1 Timothy, Paul's instructions have a broader application to Christian life, including worship outside the assembly (Bible classes, devotionals, etc.). Specific requirements for men include leading public prayer and teaching (1 Timothy 2:8, 12). But what about the women? Paul explains their role in worship in verses 9-15. The godly woman does not dress to draw attention to herself. Her appearance is modest and appropriate. She is concerned not with the external but with the inward beauty of good works as she bows her head in reverent prayer to God. She learns in quietness with all submission because "Adam was formed first, then Eve. And Adam was not deceived, but the woman, being deceived fell into transgression" (v. 14 NKJV). God loves woman, and He has a special place for her. "She [women in general] will be saved in childbearing, if they [individually] continue in faith, love, and holiness with self-control" (v. 15 NKJV). Rex Turner explains:

> The meaning is really quite simple, and further, it shines with a description of the dignity and position of the woman. The statement places the domestic life of the woman in contrast with the public life of the man. The point is that the man labors in a public role or realm for the lifting of fallen humanity; whereas, the woman labors in a private role or realm for the rise of humanity.[4]

Paul's message has a broader application than just the public assembly. Men are to lead prayers whenever Christian men and women pray together. Women's appropriate and modest dress is required in all worship/church life settings. It is practical for other times, but she is free to dress down at home and dress up, even extravagantly, for fun occasions. And women are to learn in quietness, not teaching or having authority over men when studying God's Word. Some believe Paul forbids a woman to teach or have authority over a man in any area of life. But this text seems to apply to the spiritual realm, to worship/church life settings, not the secular world. Remember Ferguson's observation: "The prohibition of exercising authority over men, ... is not a general principle applicable to any situation, but has a specific reference to the assembled church."[5] What about woman's submission in 1 Corinthians 14:34-35? Ferguson notes that "this submission ... is in the assem-

bly, not a general command for women to be subordinate to men." [6]
Can a woman teach a college English class? Can she serve as a school
superintendent? Can she be manager of a supermarket? Can she govern a city or a nation? If Paul's message applies to the secular world,
where do we draw the line? God's purpose has never been to suppress women. His restriction applies in the home and in the church.
If given a choice, many women prefer to fulfill the God-given role of
wife, mother and homemaker without the harsh and demanding pressures of leadership required of men. For those trying to maintain spiritually healthy homes while teaching and holding authoritative positions, life may be more difficult physically and emotionally than for
their male counterpart. But for those with financial need or time and
skills to work outside the home, God allows this freedom.

What about "saved in childbearing" (1 Timothy 2:15)? God designed
woman (not man) to be a loving mother, and in this sphere she can find
her greatest satisfaction. Our society has convinced many that to dedicate oneself to this task is demeaning and a waste of talent. For this,
our children are suffering terribly. God planned for fathers to fulfill
their duty in leading and providing for the family so that mothers can
focus on this very important job of mothering. Helen Andelin gives the
Christian mother's perspective.

> [She] looks with pride on her position in the home. To her it
> is a place of honor and importance. She is filling a function
> no one else can fill. Creating a happy marriage and family
> life and raising well-adjusted, honorable children are the greatest contributions she can make to the well being of society. [7]

Proverbs 31:27-28 tells us the reward for the woman who watches
over the ways of her household – "Her children rise up and call her
blessed; Her husband also, and he praises her" (NKJV). To find out if this
is true, just ask the godly older women who did.

HONOR WIDOWS WHO ARE WIDOWS INDEED (1 Timothy 5:3)

When a godly woman is old, her children (who call her blessed) will
return her love and sacrifice by providing for her needs. That is God's

plan. If she is widowed with no children to care for her, Paul commanded the church to provide. Because in the first century there were many areas where women could best serve, the church enrolled widows. These women ministered to the sick and to the needs of children and other women and were supported financially. Those too old or feeble to work contributed through an important ministry of prayer. Although the support of needy widows has not continued in the church, it is certainly an idea worth considering. These worthy women can be an excellent resource for the church in work and prayer.

LET THE YOUNGER WIDOWS MARRY
(1 Timothy 5:14-16)

Younger women could not be put on the list of supported widows. Paul encouraged them to marry, bear children and manage the house. God knew they would find more happiness there than in the restrictive life of the enrolled widow. In 1 Corinthians 7:39, Paul says she may marry "only in the Lord." Living the Christian life is much easier when one's husband walks with her. This is God's will for the widow. But if a woman is already married to an unbeliever, "let her not divorce him. For the unbelieving husband is sanctified by the wife ... how do you know, O wife, whether you will save your husband" (1 Corinthians 7:13-16 NKJV). Our loving Father provides hope through a recipe for converting the unbelieving husband (1 Peter 3:1-2).

THEY, WITHOUT A WORD, MAY BE WON
(1 Peter 3:1-2)

How can a woman convert her unbelieving or spiritually weak husband? God planned for every husband to be a strong, spiritual leader for his family. But Satan works hard at urging women to reject the leadership traits in their husbands and any attempts they make to lead. The man is different from woman in form and function. God made him that way. If a woman really wants her husband to be the leader God intended, she must understand and accept the male characteristics God placed in him. These traits help him withstand the pressures and criticism leaders must handle. If she pushes and nags, she will get friction, an empty home or a henpecked weakling.

Peter instructs them to "be submissive to your own husbands, that even if some do not obey the word, they, without a word, may be won by the conduct of their wives, when they observe your chaste conduct accompanied by fear" (1 Peter 3:1-2 NKJV). Voluntarily submitting to her husband's God-given authority, having a pure heart and mind, and showing respect for God and her spouse make up the biblical formula for changing the attitude of the unbelieving or spiritually weak husband. This will draw him to godly obedience. Her submission and encouragement will inspire confidence in his leadership efforts. Continued prayer and obedience to God will have a transforming effect on his life. It really will! Never give up.

DAUGHTERS OF SARAH (1 Peter 3:3-7)

You can be beautiful with the beauty of holiness. Peter encourages women to focus, not on external appearance, but on true beauty of the heart. He was writing to female converts who wanted to convert their husbands. Hobbs writes, "It is possible for women, by disposition and behavior, to win or fail to win others to the Lord."[8] The world values outward beauty and stylish dress. But the very precious unfading beauty of a gentle and quiet spirit is the beauty God values. That is how holy women of the past made themselves beautiful.

Sarah is our example. She respected Abraham's authority and obeyed him, even in the face of trying circumstances. We are her daughters, as spiritual children of Abraham, but only truly if we do good and do not fear any terror. We must maintain our allegiance to God first while deferring to our husband and be courageous in unjust and frightening circumstances. The *Pulpit Commentary* beautifully summarizes, "Christian women are Sarah's daughters in the faith, while they persevere in the way of holiness, and preserve a calm unruffled spirit, not easily excited, not terrified by every sudden scare, but resting in the Lord."[9]

Peter also teaches Christian husbands how to treat their wives. Unlike pagans, they must have a biblical view of marriage. The husband is to dwell with her with understanding and honor because she has a more delicate frame and because they are joint heirs together in the blessed hope of eternal life.

THE BIBLE DOES NOT AUTHORIZE THE APPOINTMENT OF DEACONESSES
(Romans 16:1; 1 Timothy 3:11)

Paul described Phoebe as a *diakonos*. This term is translated servant, minister and deacon. Which was she? Romans 16:1 proves only that Phoebe served somehow. In 1 Timothy 3:11, Paul may have been talking about female servants in his discussion of deacons. But, he may have meant deacon's wives. He did not use the term *"diakonos"* (servant, minister, deacon). He used *"gune"* (woman, wife). The only biblical examples of appointed female servants are the enrolled widows. And Paul uses only the Greek term for widow to describe them.

Historical records show no real evidence of deaconesses until the third century, and there the obscure role was the same as the enrolled widow. Fourth-century accounts show an increase in their technical status as "an order of deaconesses." This order had developed into an official position God never intended. Later religious councils terminated this unauthorized rank.

Today's world perceives the deaconess as a female deacon, officially appointed in a technical sense. We have an apparent example of the deacons' official appointment in Acts 6. But the Bible does not authorize the appointment of female servants (deaconesses) in the same way as male deacons. The world does not realize that. This is why it is unwise to give the title of deaconess to female servants in the church. Our recognition of male spiritual leadership would be obscured. As Paul told the Corinthians, the divinely established authority/submission order must be demonstrated, not concealed, in worship.

WHAT ABOUT DEBORAH?

Deborah, the prophetess, is included in this summary because she is often held up as an example of a woman leading men. Did she really lead? God commanded Barak to go up into battle, but the man did not want the responsibility of leadership. He asked for help from the spiritually superior Deborah. She knew God's plan was for Barak to lead, and that is exactly what she encouraged him to do. She did not take the leadership role. "And Barak called Zebulun and Naphtali to Kedesh; he went up with ten thousand men under his command, and

Deborah went up with him" (Judges 4:10 NKJV). She helped Barak the best way she could. She went with him but allowed him to remain in authority. She did not take his leadership role.

Cecil May Jr. told a story at the Faulkner Lectureship about a congregation made up mostly of women. The few men who occasionally attended refused to lead. To retain God's authority/submission order, a man will stand before the congregation to lead singing. One godly woman near the front row remains in her seat and humbly helps him start the first notes. She does not stand up and act as the song leader. She remains in a submissive position while encouraging and helping him fulfill his responsibility. Like Deborah, she is a submissive servant who encourages the male spiritual leadership God requires. The women of this congregation conduct themselves as submissive servants. They understand that male spiritual leadership must be demonstrated in worship. And they do the best they can to ensure that authority/submission order is clearly seen. How pleased must God be with this church!

WHAT ABOUT THE WOMEN TODAY?

Many first-century women reading God's inspired messages were coming out of pagan lifestyles and needed instruction on Christlike behavior. But these timeless instructions are relevant today. The New Testament scriptures about women are filled with reminders of the divinely established authority/submission order.

In the home, it is still not good for man to be alone. He is incomplete physically and emotionally. We are called, as wives, to recognize the husband's authority as head of the home.

God planned for husbands to bear the heaviest responsibilities, and they are commanded to love us sacrificially. With this kind of atmosphere, we are free to focus on our responsibilities to manage our homes creatively and lovingly raise our children in the Lord. And what joy we have when this is accomplished!

In the church, God also requires male spiritual leadership. This pleases Him. The ignorant say this reduces women to second-class Christians. Forced submission would do that. But God does not command men to force submission upon women. He asks women to subordinate voluntarily themselves and allow His authority/submission order to be seen. The ignorant cry, "A church dominated by men only will find itself a source of scandal."[10] Does this mean Christians must ignore God's commands to win approval from the world? Some cry, "Women should be allowed to use their talents in the Lord's service!" Yes, they should! Are women not using their talents when they teach God's Word to other women and children, when they minister to the sick, visit the prisons, take food to the shut-ins, gather clothing for the needy, console the bereaved, sing at weddings and funerals, decorate for vacation Bible school, knock doors and pass out tracts for gospel meetings, and encourage others? And the list could go on and on. Our talents can be used! There are so many wonderful areas of service in which women can and should participate, especially in the neglected training of younger women (Titus 2:3-5). Sheila Keckler Butt notes:

> Ironically, many women are clamoring for leadership roles in the worship services but have virtually overlooked this passage of Scripture…. We should not be nearly as concerned with changing women's roles in the church as we are with discharging the roles God has given us.[11]

If the older women teach the younger women how to have spiritually healthy lives and homes, men will learn to lead and children will learn to respect authority! We can have spiritually healthy homes, churches and communities.

But we must not set aside the one restriction God has placed upon us. Eve suffered greatly for making that terrible mistake. We can count our many blessings and see our role in the proper perspective. Ferguson observes:

> This [created order] carries no implication of inferiority for women nor of negative judgment on women's ability. Any given woman may be the spiritual or intellectual superior of any given man. The designated roles are signs pointing to something more fundamental: that God is God and human beings are his creatures who must respect his institutions.[12]

Ladies, this book is an urgent plea for us to reconsider God's call for submissive service. It is not forced upon us, nor is it an infringement on our equality. It is a love-initiated response to the needs of others – in our homes, in our churches, in our communities, in our world. And our godly response to these needs is urgent! Through the avenue God has given us, we encourage male leadership, we attract others to Christ, and we reverently serve our Lord. What about the women? Frankly, it's not about us. It's about Him. He has called us to a special purpose. If we desire heaven, we must humbly comply.

Questions

1. Discuss the impact on our society if older women teach and younger women learn how to have spiritually healthy families.

2. Compare the biblical view of the wife's submission with Satan's deceptive view.

3. Why did Paul tell the Corinthian women to retain their veils in worship? How does this apply today?

4. What was the basis for women's silence in the assembly in 1 Corinthians 14:34-35? Does culture affect that basis?

5. Discuss Rex Turner's comparison of a woman's realm in childbearing as a labor for the rise of humanity and the man's realm in the lifting of fallen humanity.

6. Discuss benefits that praying and ministering widows could have for a congregation who supports them.

7. Why did Paul advise the younger widows to marry?

8. Compare the effects of the wife who encourages her husband's leadership with the wife who criticizes her husband for his lack of it.

9. Discuss the impact that a Christian woman's meek and quiet spirit can have on unbelievers.

10. How would you answer a woman who wants to be called a deaconess?

Endnotes

Chapter 1

1 Dewey Fogerson, "Instructions Concerning Various Groups: (Titus 2:1-15)," *Studies in Timothy and Titus*, ed. David Lipe (Knoxville, Tenn.: East Tennessee School of Preaching and Missions, 1986) 260.

2 Adam Clarke, *Commentary on the Holy Bible* (Grand Rapids, Mich.: Baker Book House, 1967) 1241.

3 Gordon Fee, *Timothy and Titus* (Peabody, Mass.: Hendrickson Pub., 1988) 186.

4 Fee, 186.

5 M. Lynn Gannett, "Older Women/ Younger Women: The Implementation of Titus 2" *The Christian Educator's Handbook on Family Life Education*, eds. Kenneth O. Gangel and James C. Wilhoit (Wheaton, Ill.: Victor Books, 1993) 90.

6 Gannett, 89.

7 Fee, 187.

8 Fogerson, 261.

Chapter 2

1 James Burton Coffman, *Commentary on 1 & 2 Thessalonians, 1 & 2 Timothy, Titus & Philemon*. James Burton Coffman Commentary Series (Austin, Texas: Firm Foundation, 1978) 334.

2 T. Pierce Brown, "Teaching Love," *Gospel Advocate*, 3 Feb. 1983: 70.

3 Ross Campbell, *How To Really Love Your Child* (Wheaton, Ill.: Victor Books, 1983) back cover.

4 Campbell, 41.

5 Albert Barnes, *Barnes' Notes on the New Testament* (Grand Rapids, Mich.: Kregel Pub., 1962) 1195.

6 Tom Holland, "The Role of Women," *Studies in Timothy and Titus*, ed. David Lipe, (Knoxville, Tenn.: East Tennessee School of Preaching and Missions, 1986) 313.

7 Bruce M. Metzger, *A Textual Commentary on the Greek New Testament* (New York: United Bible Societies, 1994) 585. The King James translation was made from the original word "*oikourous*" (those of the home), but it has since been shown that *oikourgous* (*oikos* – house and ergous – workers) is the better word. Metzger cites, "A majority of the Committee preferred the latter reading because of superior external support, and because it was regarded more probable that an unusual word should have been altered by copyists to a well-known word, than vice versa."

8 Sybil Stanton, *The 25-Hour Woman* (Old Tappan, N.J.: Fleming H. Revell Co., 1986) 46.

9 Helen B. Andelin, *Fascinating Womanhood*, rev. ed. (Santa Barbara, Calif.: Pacific Press, 1974) 201.

10 Andelin, 202-203.

11 Brenda Hunter, *The Power of Mother Love* (Colorado Springs, Colo.: WaterBrook Press, 1997) 54.

12 Barnes, *Notes* 1195.

13 Warren W. Wiersbe, *Be Faithful* (Wheaton, Ill.: Victor Books, 1981) 33-34.

Chapter 3

1 F. LaGard Smith, *Male Spiritual Leadership* (Nashville: 21st Century Christian, 1998) 28-29. I am indebted to F. LaGard Smith for ideas on male spiritual leadership from his book, *Male Spiritual Leadership*.

2 Smith, 29.

3 John L. Kachelman refers to these as "the first born rule" and "the authority of source" in his article, "The Rationale for Women's Subjection," *Christian Bible Teacher*, Jan. 1993: 20. He also lists the power of naming and the principle of provision.

4 Smith, 39.

5 Smith, 56.

6 John Mark Hicks and Bruce L. Morton, *Woman's Role in the Church* (Shreveport, La.: Lambert Book House, 1978) 10-11. They cite the reality of work and childbearing both made more difficult after the fall and conclude that the reality of man's authority was adversely affected also.

7 Kachelman, 20.

8 Dave Miller, "Women in the Church: An Exegesis of 1 Timothy 2:11-15" (a paper presented at the Lubbock Christian University Lectureship, Oct. 1991) 11.

9 Hicks and Morton call this the authority-subordination principle, 36.

10 William Hendriksen, *New Testament Commentary, Exposition of the Pastoral Epistles* (Grand Rapids: Baker Book House, 1957) 110.

11 Smith, 54.

12 John Piper, "Satan's Design in Reversing Male Leadership Role," *The Standard* 73 (Dec. 1983): 33, quoted in Miller, 10.

13 Smith, 31.

14 Jo Berry, *Beloved Unbeliever* (Grand Rapids, Mich.: Zondervan, 1981) 101-102.

Chapter 4

1 F. LaGard Smith, *Male Spiritual Leadership* (Nashville: 21st Century Christian, 1998) 137.

2   Everett Ferguson writes, "They are found as physicians, musicians, artists, winners of athletic events, selling groceries, and in all sorts of manufacturing and commercial activities." Everett Ferguson, *Backgrounds of Early Christianity*, 2d ed. (Grand Rapids: Eerdmans, 1993), 72.

3   William Barclay, *The Letters to the Corinthians*, 2d ed. (Philadelphia: Westminster Press, 1956), 109.

4   Lawrence O. Richards, *Expository Dictionary of Biblical Words*, 1985 ed., s.v. "Head: in 1 Cor. 11."

5   Gordon D. Fee, *The First Epistle to the Corinthians* (Grand Rapids: Eerdmans, 1987. Fee explains, "Given the combative nature of so much of his response, it seems highly likely that in their letter they have taken considerable exception to several of his positions and/or prohibitions." (7).

6   Carroll D. Osburn, "1 Cor. 11:2-16 – Public or Private?" in *Essays on Women in Earliest Christianity* (Joplin, Mo.: College Press, 1993): 316.

7   Roy Deaver, "Difficult Texts From First and Second Corinthians: 1 Cor. 11:1-16, Women and Veils," in *Difficult Texts of the New Testament Explained*: The Fourth Annual Fort Worth Christian Lectures. ed. Wendell Winkler, (Winkler Publications, Box 17631, Montgomery, Ala., 1981), 270.

8   Bauer's *Greek-English Lexicon of the New Testament and Other Early Christian Literature*, 1979 ed., s.v. "ekklasia."

9   Everett Ferguson, *Women in the Church* (Chickashaw, Okla.: Yeoman Press, 2003), 26.

10 Fee, 497-98.

11 Bauer, s.v. "kata."

12 A.T. Robertson and Alfred Plummer, *A Critical and Exegetical Commentary on the First Epistle of St. Paul to the Corinthians*, 2d ed. (Edinburgh, Scotland: T & T Clark, 1967) 229.

13 Ferguson, *Women* 22.

14 Bruce K. Waltke, "1 Corinthians 11:2-16: An Interpretation," *Bibliotheca Sacra* (Jan.-Mar. 1978): 51. Waltke suggests the woman without her head covering dishonored her own (literal) head by appearing in a culturally disgraceful manner.

15 Robertson, 231.

16 Waltke, 49.

17 Waltke, 51.

18 *Theological Dictionary of the New Testament*, 1964 ed. s.v. "doxa."

19 Warren W. Wiersbe, *The Bible Exposition Commentary*, vol. 1 (Wheaton, Ill.: Victor Books, 1989) 604.

20 Wayne Jackson, "Command or Culture?" *Spiritual Sword* 25 (April 1, 1994): 28-33.

Chapter 5

1   Bruce K. Waltke, "1 Corinthians 11:2-16: An Interpretation," *Bibliotheca Sacra* (Jan.-Mar. 1978): 56-57.

2   F. LaGard Smith, *Male Spiritual Leadership* (Nashville: 21st Century Christian, 1998) 234.

3 W. Gerald Kendrick, "Authority, Women, and Angels: Translating 1 Corinthians 11:10," *The Bible Translator*, 46. 3 (July 1995) 336.

4 Sir William Ramsey, *The Cities of St. Paul: Their Influence on His Life and Thought*, London 1907; reprint Grand Rapids: Baker 1960, 203-05; quoted in William Barclay, *The Letters to the Corinthians*, 2d. ed (Philadelphia: The Westminster Press, 1956) 108-109.

5 Albert Barnes, *Barnes' Notes on the New Testament* (Grand Rapids, Mich.: Kregel Pub., 1962) 755.

6 Gordon D. Fee, *First Epistle to the Corinthians* (Grand Rapids, Mich.: Eerdmans, 1989) 521.

7 F.W. Farrar, *The Pulpit Commentary: Corinthians*, vol. 19, H.D.M. Spence and Joseph S. Exell, eds. (Grand Rapids, Mich: Eerdmans, 1975), 362.

8 A.T. Robertson and Alfred Plummer, *A Critical and Exegetical Commentary on the First Epistle of St. Paul to the Corinthians*, 2d ed. (Edinburgh, Scotland: T & T Clark, 1967) 233.

9 *Pulpit*, 363.

10 Barnes, *Notes* 755.

11 James Burton Coffman, *First & Second Corinthians,* James Burton Coffman Commentary Series (Austin, Texas: Firm Foundation, 1977) 174.

12 William Barclay, *The Letters to the Corinthians*, 2d ed. (Philadelphia: Westminster Press, 1956) 110.

13 A.T. Robertson and Alfred Plummer, *Critical and Exegetical Commentary on the First Epistle of St. Paul to the Corinthians* (Edinburgh, Scotland: T & T Clark, 1914, 2nd ed.) 233.

14 Dan R. Owen, "An Exegesis of Three Texts Regarding the Role of Women in the Church," *Gospel Advocate* Feb. 2004: 36.

15 Dan Owen E-mail to author. 12 Oct. 2004. See also *The Apocrypha and Pseudepigrapha of the Old Testament in English*, ed. R.H. Charles, vol. II, p. 188.

16 Kenneth T. Wilson, "Should Women Wear Head coverings?" *Bibliotheca Sacra* Oct.-Dec. 1991: 442.

17 Coffman, *1 Timothy* 333-34.

18 Robertson, 234.

19 Warren W. Wiersbe, *The Bible Exposition Commentary*, vol. 1 (Wheaton, Ill.: Victor Books, 1989) 604.

20 Rick Simmons, "The Teaching of 1 Corinthians 11:2-16 and 14:34-36 on the Role of Women in Public Worship" (unpublished paper Summer 1990); quoted in Wilson, 461.

21 Wiersbe, *Commentary* 604.

Chapter 6

1 Bruce M. Metzger, *A Textual Commentary on the Greek New Testament* (New York: United Bible Societies, 1994) King James and New King James add the word "your," but the latest Greek texts omit that word. When the word "your" appeared, it generally signaled that *gunay* meant "wives." The NKJV makes a note: NU omits your. Metzger (500) notes, "The Textus Receptus, following D F G K L many minuscules

it [d,g syrp,h with obelus] al, reads υμων after gunaikes. The Committee regarded this a probably a scribal addition, and preferred the shorter text."

2 Everett Ferguson, *Women in the Church* (Chickashaw, Okla.: Yeoman Press, 2003) 11-21.

3 Walter Bauer, *A Greek-English Lexicon of the New Testament and Other Early Christian Literature*, ed. Frederick W. Danker (Chicago: University of Chicago Press, 1979)

4 Ferguson, *Women* 15.

5 Kenneth T. Wilson, "Should Women Wear Head coverings?" *Bibliotheca Sacra* Oct.-Dec. 1991: 37.

6 Ferguson, *Women* 11.

7 Bauer, s.v. *"laleo."*

8 F. LaGard Smith, *Male Spiritual Leadership* (Nashville: 21st Century Christian, 1998) 113.

9 Ferguson, *Women* 17.

10 The same word is translated "women" in 1 Timothy 2:9-12, 14, and "wife" in 1 Timothy 3:2, 12; 5:9.

11 Everett and Nancy Ferguson, "The Assembly – 1 Corinthians 14," *Gospel Advocate,* Sept. 1993: 10.

12 Ferguson, *Women* 19.

13 Bauer, s.v. *"nomos."*

14 Cecil May Jr. "In Accordance With God's Word," *Gospel Advocate* Jan. 2004: 13.

15 Everett and NancyFerguson, "New Testament Teaching on the Role of Women in the Assembly," *Gospel Advocate* Oct. 1990: 30.

16 Everett and Nancy Ferguson, "In Subjection to God" *Gospel Advocate* Jan. 2004: 23.

17 Daniel C. Arichea Jr., "The Silence of Women in the Church: Theology and Translation in 1 Corinthians 14:33b-36," *The Bible Translator* 46 (Jan. 1995): 103. The ASV, in 1902, made 33a a sentence and connected 33b with what follows. This is also true in the RSV, TEV, NEB, the CEV. *The Greek New Testament*, 3d. ed. (Federal Republic of Germany: United Bible Societies, 1983).

18 Arichea, 102-03.

19 Ferguson, *Women,* says, "The New Revised Standard Version and New International Version (as others) are probably correct in construing this clause with what follows in verse 34 rather than with what precedes in verse 33," 18.

20 Bauer, s.v. *"ekklasia."*

21 Warren W. Wiersbe, *The Bible Exposition Commentary*, vol. 1 (Wheaton, Ill.: Victor Books, 1989) 616.

Chapter 7

1 Dave Miller, "Women in the Church: An Exegesis of 1 Timothy 2:11-15" (a paper presented at the Lubbock Christian University Lectureship, Oct. 1991) 2.

2 Everett Ferguson,"Topos in 1 Timothy 2:8," *Restoration Quarterly* 33 (1991): 65-73.

3 Miller, 2.

4 Cecil May Jr. "In Accordance With God's Word," *Gospel Advocate* Jan. 2004:13.

5 J.W. Roberts, *The Living Word, Letters to Timothy* (Austin: R.B. Sweet, 1964) 21.

6 A.C. Hervey, *The Pulpit Commentary: 1 Timothy*, vol. 21, H.D.M. Spence and Joseph S. Exell, eds., (Grand Rapids: Eerdmans, 1962) 40-41.

7 Charles Crouch, "Proper Apparel in Divine Worship," *Gospel Advocate* 5 April 1984: 206.

8 David Roper, "The Christian and Immodest Apparel" *Gospel Advocate* 19 June 1986: 369-370.

9 William Hendriksen, *New Testament Commentary, Exposition of the Pastoral Epistles* (Grand Rapids: Baker Book House, 1957) 107.

10 Charles Crouch, "The Case for Modest Apparel," *Gospel Advocate* 16 Sept. 1982: 564.

11 ySotah 3.19a; quoted in Everett Ferguson, *Women in the Church* (Chickashaw, Okla.: Yeoman Press, 2003) 33.

12 Scot McKnight, *The NIV Application Commentary: 1 Peter*, Terry Muck, gen. ed. (Grand Rapids: Zondervan, 1996) 183.

13 "Silence" in 1 Corinthians 14 is from *sigao*. "Quietness" in 1 Timothy 2 is from *hesuchia*.

14 Jack P. Lewis, "Quietness or Silence" *Gospel Advocate* July 1988: 11-12.

15 Everett and Nancy Ferguson, "In Subjection to God" *Gospel Advocate* Jan. 2004: 23. In *Women* (33), Ferguson says en *husuchia* "refers to a state of quietness without disturbance but, although a different word from 'silence' in 1 Corinthians 14, can have that meaning in some contexts (cf. Acts 22:2; and one manuscript of 21:40 instead of sige)."

16 Walter Bauer, *A Greek-English Lexicon of the New Testament and Other Early Christian Literature*, ed. Frederick W. Danker (Chicago: University of Chicago Press, 1979) s.v. "*aner*."

17 Christopher R. Hutson, *My True Child: The Rhetoric of Youth in the Pastoral Epistles*, diss., Yale U, 1998.

18 David Warren, Ph.D. Harvard, E-Mail to author. 27 Jan. 2004.

19 Ferguson, *Women* 34.

20 Hendriksen, 110.

21 Roberts, 23.

22 Guy N. Woods, "Saved Through Childbearing," *Gospel Advocate* Dec. 1976: 774.

23 Warren W. Wiersbe, *The Bible Exposition Commentary*, vol. 2 (Wheaton, Ill.: Victor Books, 1989) 216

24 Hendriksen, 111.

25 Ferguson, *Women* 36.

Chapter 8

1 Joanne Howe, *A Change of Habit: the Autobiography of a Former Catholic Nun* (Nashville: Christian Communications, 1986).

2 *International Standard Bible Encyclopedia*, s.v. "deaconess."

3 Albert Barnes, *Barnes' Notes on the New Testament* (Grand Rapids, Mich.: Kregel Pub., 1962) 1152.

4 A.C. Hervey, *The Pulpit Commentary: 1 Timothy*, vol. 21, H.D.M. Spence and Joseph S. Exell, eds., (Grand Rapids: Eerdmans, 1962) 110.

5 *Pulpit, 1 Timothy* 111.
6 Warren W. Wiersbe, *The Bible Exposition Commentary*, vol. 1 (Wheaton, Ill.: Victor Books, 1989) 742.
7 Barnes, *Notes* 1152.
8 William Barclay, *The Letters to Timothy, Titus, & Philemon*, 2d. ed. (Philadelphia: The Westminster Press, 1960) 123-24.
9 Barclay, *Timothy* 124.
10 *Pulpit, 1 Timothy* 112.
11 Warren W. Wiersbe, *Be Faithful* (Wheaton, Ill.: Victor Books, 1981) 69.
12 Everett Ferguson, *Women in the Church* (Chickashaw, Okla.: Yeoman Press, 2003) 47.
13 Ferguson, *Women,* 47
14 Gordon Fee, *Timothy and Titus* (Peabody, Mass.: Hendrickson Pub., 1988) 186.
15 Wiersbe, *Faithful* 70.
16 J.W. Roberts, *The Living Word, Letters to Timothy* (Austin: R.B. Sweet, 1964) 58.
17 Barclay, *Timothy* 127-28.
18 Everett Ferguson, *The Church of Christ: A Biblical Ecclesiology for Today* (Grand Rapids: Eerdmans, 1996) 340.

Chapter 9

1 Warren W. Wiersbe, *The Bible Exposition Commentary*, vol. 2 (Wheaton, Ill.: Victor Books, 1989) 743.
2 William Hendriksen, *New Testament Commentary, Exposition of the Pastoral Epistles* (Grand Rapids: Baker Book House, 1957) 175.
3 Hendriksen, 178.
4 June Wesley, "A Lonely Widow" *20th Century Christian* 51 (1 April 1989): 18.
5 John F. Walvoord and Roy B. Zuck, *The Bible Knowledge Commentary: New Testament Edition* (Colorado Springs, Colo.: Cook Communications, 1983) 520.
6 Burton Coffman, *First and Second Corinthians*, vol 7, James Burton Coffman Commentary Series (1974, copyright assigned to ACU Press, 1984) 116.
7 David Lipscomb, edited with additional notes by J.W. Shepherd, *A Commentary on the New Testament Epistles: First Corinthians*, vol. 2, (Nashville: Gospel Advocate, 1968) 115-16.
8 Jim McGuiggan, *The Book of 1 Corinthians*, Looking Into the Bible Series, (Lubbock, Texas: Montex, 1984) 118-19.
9 James Meadows, "The Widow and 'in the Lord' (1 Corinthians 7:39)," Freed-Hardeman University Lectures, vol. 46, 1 Feb. 1982: 273-74. Meadows (274-275) cites Roy Deaver, Biblical Notes, vol. XIV, Dec. 1980 (127-28) and Rubel Shelly, Notes, 30 March 1978.
10 R.C.H. Lenski, *Interpretation of St. Paul's First and Second Epistles to the Corinthians,* Commentary on the New Testament, (Peabody, Mass.:Hendrickson Publishers Edition, 1937, 1963) 331.
11 Meadows, 276.

Chapter 10

1 Steve Farrar, *Point Man* (Portland, Ore.: Multnomah Press, 1990) 20-21.
2 Barbara Johnson, *Living Somewhere Between Estrogen and Death* (Dallas: Word, 1997) 139.
3 Tim LaHaye, *Understanding the Male Temperament* (Old Tappan, N.J.: Fleming H. Revell, 1977) 22-23.
4 Jo Berry, *Beloved Unbeliever* (Grand Rapids, Mich.: Zondervan, 1981) 45.
5 Scot McKnight, *The NIV Application Commentary: 1 Peter*, Terry Muck, gen. ed. (Grand Rapids: Zondervan, 1996) 183.
6 McKnight, 184.
7 Janell Smitherman, "Praise Your Husband into Greatness," *Christian Woman* Nov./Dec. 2001: 21.
8 Smitherman, 21.
9 Smitherman, 21.
10 Helen B. Andelin, *Fascinating Womanhood*, rev. ed. (Santa Barbara, Calif.: Pacific Press, 1974) 40-43.
11 LaHaye, 22.
12 John F. Walvoord and Roy B. Zuck, *The Bible Knowledge Commentary: New Testament Edition* (Colorado Springs, Colo.: Cook Communications, 1983) 848.
13 McKnight, 183.
14 Berry, 46.
15 J. Ramsey Michaels, *Word Biblical Commentary: 1 Peter*, vol. 49 (Waco, Texas: Word, 1988) 158.
16 Jane Kirby Smith, "The Unbelieving Husband" *Christian Family*, Jan. 1985: 7.
17 Billye Christian, "Faith of a Sunday Morning Widow" *Christian Bible Teacher*, Feb. 2000: 33.

Chapter 11

1 J. Ramsey Michaels, *Word Biblical Commentary: 1 Peter*, vol. 49 (Waco, Texas: Word, 1988) 160.
2 Lottie Beth Hobbs, *You Can Be Beautiful With the Beauty of Holiness* (Fort Worth, Texas: Harvest Publications, 1959) forward.
3 Michaels, 161.
4 J.N.D. Kelly, *A Commentary on the Epistles of Peter and Jude* (Grand Rapids: Baker Book House, 1981) 129.
5 Kelly, 129.
6 J.W. Roberts, *The Living Word: 1 & 2 Peter and Jude* (Austin, Texas: Sweet Pub., 1964) 38.
7 McKnight, 185.
8 Michaels, 163-64.
9 Slaughter, James R. "Instructions to Christian Wives in 1 Peter 3:1-6, Part 3," *Bibliotheca Sacra 153* (July-Sept. 1996): 358.
10 Michaels, 164.
11 James Burton Coffman, *James, 1 & 2 Peter, 1, 2 & 3 John, Jude,* James Burton Coffman Commentary Series (Austin, Texas: Firm Foundation, 1979) 219.

12 Kelly, 131. Slaughter (361) emphasizes the conditional aspect.

13 Michaels, 167.

14 B.C. Caffin, *The Pulpit Commentary: 1 Peter*, vol. 22, H.D.M. Spence and Joseph S. Exell, eds., (Grand Rapids, Mich.: Eerdmans, 1950) 129.

15 *Pulpit*, 1 Peter, 138.

16 Fred B. Craddock, *First and Second Peter and Jude* (Louisville, Ky.: Westminster John Knox Press, 1995) 52.

17 *Pulpit*, 1 Peter, 138.

18 Edwin A. Blum, *The Expositor's Bible Commentary: 1 Peter*, vol 12, Frank E. Gaebelein, gen. ed., (Grand Rapids: Zondervan, 1981) 237.

19 Kelly, *"skeuos,"* 133.

20 Albert Barnes, *Barnes' Notes on the New Testament* (Grand Rapids, Mich.: Kregel Pub., 1962) 1417.

Chapter 12

1 Willard Collins, "Women Assuming Leadership Roles," *Gospel Advocate* Feb. 1992: 25.

2 *MSN Encarta Encyclopedia*, s.v. "deaconess," <http://www.encarta.msn.com/dictionary_/deaconess> 30 Sept. 2004.

3 Everett Ferguson, *The Church of Christ: A Biblical Ecclesiology for Today* (Grand Rapids: Eerdmans, 1996) 338.

4 Guy N. Woods, *Questions and Answers,* vol. II (Nashville: Gospel Advocate, 1986: 173.

5 J. Stephen Sandifer, *Deacons: Male and Female?* (Houston, Texas: By the Author, 1989), 42-3. Sandifer lists scholars holding that 1 Timothy 3:11 refers to wives of deacons: A. Barnes, R.M. Gromacki, W.W. Wiersbe, and others.

6 Warren W. Wiersbe, *Be Faithful* (Wheaton, Ill.: Victor Books, 1981) 48.

7 Marvin R. Vincent, *Word Studies in the New Testament* (Grand Rapids, Mich.: Eerdmans, 1973) 236.

8 James Burton Coffman, *Commentary on 1 & 2 Thessalonians, 1 & 2 Timothy, Titus & Philemon.* James Burton Coffman Commentary Series (Austin, Texas: Firm Foundation, 1978) 183.

9 Sandifer lists scholars in favor of 1 Timothy 3:11 as being qualifications for female "deacons": W. Barclay, F.F. Bruce, C.E. Cerling, J. Chrysostrom, A.C. Hervey, J.N.D. Kelly, R.C.H. Lenski, J.B. Lightfoot, W. Lock, and others, 42. He also lists those uncertain of the interpretation and those uncertain, but leaning toward "deaconess": C.K. Barrett, A.T. Robinson, and others, and those uncertain, but leaning toward "wives": M.R. Vincent and others, 43.

10 Ferguson, *Church* 339.

11 Ferguson, *Church* 339.

12 William Barclay, *The Letters to Timothy, Titus, & Philemon*, 2d. ed. (Philadelphia: The Westminster Press, 1960) 99.

13 Robert R. Taylor Jr., "Difficult Texts From 1 and 2 Timothy and Titus," *Difficult Texts of the New Testament Explained*, ed. Wendell Winkler (Hurst, Texas: Winkler Pub., 1981) 324.

14 W.E. Vine, *Vine's Expository Dictionary of New Testament Words*, eds, Merrill F. Unger and William White Jr., (Nashville: Thomas Nelson, 1968) s.v. "Deacon."

15 Ferguson, *Women* 47.

16 *Interpreter's Dictionary of the Bible*, (Nashville: Abingdon Press, 1962) "Deaconess."

17 *New Advent,* Catholic Encyclopedia On-Line <http://www.newadvent.org/cathen/04651a.htm>. 10 Sept. 2004.

18 Everett Ferguson, *Women in the Church* (Chickashaw, Okla.: Yeoman Press, 2003) 48.

19 Sandifer, 128. *MSN Encarta Encyclopedia* <http://www.encarta.msn.com/dictionary_/deaconess>. 10 Sept. 2004.

20 *New Advent* Catholic Encyclopedia On-Line <http://www.newadvent.org/cathen/04651a.htm>. 10 Sept. 2004.

21 *International Standard Bible Encyclopedia,* s.v. "Deaconess."

22 Sandifer, 86-87.

23 *New Advent* Catholic Encyclopedia On-Line <http://www.newadvent.org/cathen/04651a.htm>. 10 Sept. 2004.

24 *ISBE*, s.v. "Deaconess."

25 *New Advent* Catholic Encyclopedia On-Line <http://www.newadvent.org/ca then/04651a.htm ; 10 Sept. 2004.

26 Sandifer, 92.

27 Coffman, *1 Timothy* 184.

28 Gus Nichols, "Queries Answers" *Gospel Advocate* 16 Dec. 1971: 797-98.

29 Carrol R. Sutton, "Does the New Testament Authorize Deaconesses?" *Guardian of Truth* 33 (16 Nov. 1989): 692.

30 Owen D. Olbricht, "Was Phoebe a Deaconess?" *Truth for Today* 18 (1 Dec. 1997): 19.

31 Robert R. Taylor Jr., *Studies in First and Second Timothy* (Shreveport: Lambert Book House, n.d.) 45.

32 Guy N. Woods, *Adult Gospel Quarterly* (Spring Quarter, 1978) 27.

33 Woods, *Adult* 27.

34 Wiersbe, *Faithful* 49.

35 Sandifer, 35.

Chapter 13

1 Rick Simmons, "The Teaching of 1 Corinthians 11:2-16 and 14:34-36 on the Role of Women in Public Worship" (unpublished paper Summer 1990); quoted in Wilson, 461.

2 Everett and Nancy Ferguson, "New Testament Teaching on the Role of Women in the Assembly," *Gospel Advocate* Oct. 1990: 30.

3 Everett and Nancy Ferguson, "In Subjection to God" *Gospel Advocate* Jan. 2004: 23.

4 Rex Turner Sr. "The Place of Woman in the Will of God (1 Corinthians 11:3, 8-9; 14:33-35)" *Studies in 1 Corinthians.* ed. Dub McClish (Denton, Texas: First Annual Denton Lectures) 141.

5 Everett Ferguson, *Women in the Church* (Chickashaw, Okla.: Yeoman Press, 2003) 34.

6 Ferguson, *Women* 19.

7 Helen B. Andelin, *Fascinating Womanhood*, rev. ed. (Santa Barbara, Calif.: Pacific Press, 1974) 200.

8 Lottie Beth Hobbs, *You Can Be Beautiful* (Fort Worth, Texas: Harvest, 1959) 33.

9 H.D.M. Spence and Joseph S. Exell, eds., *The Pulpit Commentary:Peter, John, Jude, and The Revelation*, vol. 22 (Grand Rapids, Mich.: Eerdmans, 1962) 138.

10 Robert M. Randolph, "Why Women Should Be Preaching in the Churches of Christ," *Leaven: A Journal in Christian Ministry*, 11.4 (Malibu, Calif.: Pepperdine University, 2003) 206

11 Sheila Keckler Butt, "The Missing Ingredient of Titus 2," *Gospel Advocate* Oct. 1995: 40.

12 Everett Ferguson, *The Church of Christ: A Biblical Ecclesiology for Today* (Grand Rapids: Eerdmans, 1996) 344